D0752253

101 Ways To Facilitate Making Friends:

How to Engage and Deepen Support Networks for People with Disabilities.

Aaron Johannes, Jim Reynolds
and Susan Stanfield
Foreword by David Pitonyak

Spectrum Press

A DIVISION OF SPECTRUM SOCIETY
FOR COMMUNITY LIVING

Copyright Spectrum Society

All rights reserved

Spectrum Press, Vancouver, B.C.: 2011

ISBN 978-1-257-06050-4

To two of our greatest teachers about real friendship:
in memory of
Arnold Bennington, President, B.C. People First
and to Randy Saul

"Remember there's no such thing
as a small act of kindness.
Every act creates a ripple with no logical end."

Scott Adams

Contents

Diesel

5

Foreword: "Ours is a Social Brain"

David Pitonyak

Ours is a social brain. When we are connected to meaningful and enduring relationships, we are significantly more likely to live longer and happier lives. We are less likely to get sick when we are connected to others and, if we do get sick, we get better faster. We are less likely to experience mental health issues. If we need to take medication, we are more likely to take it as prescribed when we are in relationship with others. We sleep better and have fewer problem behaviors. In short, we are hot wired to belong.

Many people who experience disabilities are lonely. Some, since childhood, have been cut off from their primary relationships, sent away to institutions in the name of treatment. Others, growing up at home, have been systematically disenfranchised from their communities, sent away to separate schools, separate workplaces, separate recreational activities, even separate services at church – all in the name of 'treatment' (aka: habilitation, 'being with your own kind', 'what's best', etc).

I believe that the root cause of most suffering is loneliness. Not just in the lives of people who experience disabilities, but in all people. It is not the only cause of suffering, just the most common. And everything that is separate must be healed.

In short, we are hot wired to belong.

That's why I am so delighted to write a few words about Aaron, Jim and Susan's book, 101 Ways to Make Friends: A Facilitator's Manual About How to Engage and Deepen Support Networks for People with Disabilities and Their Supporters. *Created with the help of self-advocates across British Columbia,* 101 Ways to Make Friends… *is a practical, fun, and inspired way to get started in the work of helping people to connect to meaningful and enduring relationships.*

What I love most about 101 Ways… is that it is not just a book about finding friends. It is a book about being a friend. It is not just a book about finding friends in everyday community places. It is about learning ways to make a contribution to community. Being a good friend or neighbor, son or daughter, brother or sister, aunt or uncle, partner in life. Giving as well as getting. Our social brains love it when we are needed in real ways by other members of the 'pack.'

Good luck in this work you are undertaking. It is all at once practical and groundbreaking.

David

David Pitonyak, Ph.D.,
Imagine, Blacksburg, Virginia
www.dimagine.com.

"One day I will find the right words,
and they will be simple."

Jack Kerouac (The Dharma Bums)

Introduction

When we began our original project to look at the personal networks of people with disabilities, we had no idea that we were embarking on something so transformational to everything we do and are and aspire to be. We thought it was an interesting idea, and it was under a mandate organized by Community Living British Columbia (C.L.B.C. - the funding source in our province, the result of the advocacy and work of many families, advocates and self-advocates) that had to do with Safeguards – and this interested us: the idea that having friends and family around individuals with disabilities kept them safer...

It seemed self-evident when we considered it, and, importantly, we did stop to consider it. This "stop" was really the result of work by Jule Hopkins, to whom we owe so much. And from that stop, we've undergone a journey that has led us to meet some amazing leaders in our field, and to become stewards of a conversation which has been greeted

free

9

with excitement in so many places. It was more than a year later, having dinner with John Lord and Peggy Hutchinson, that John said to us, "It's all really about seeing everything we do through a lens of relationship," and it was yet another moment of realising that a) we'd come a long way, b) we were not alone and c) we were increasingly grounded in a new vision.

At that table that night were some incredible "hosts" – John, Peggy, Barb Goode, an amazing self-advocate who has become a great friend, Jule, Shelley Nessman who is such an important resource to so many, Kim Lyster who has done so much great work around the province in so many partnerships. People were having a great time – the conversation was loud and excited, yet people were listening carefully, they were remembering together, they were open to welcoming, they were appreciative of each other, they were gentle with each other's flaws…

In our quarter-century of providing services to individuals with disabilities we've all worked hard and been relatively successful in an always-challenging field. We've also been certain for a long while that the support that's important to us and our growth comes from those we organize services for, their families and friends. And we had lots of evidence, once we stopped to consider it, that communities of caring supporters around these individuals ensured not just their safety, but that their services were as good as we wanted them to be, in ways that no kind of monitoring could replicate. One of the first calls I took as a new manager of one of the first community based day services for people with significant challenges, two decades ago, was from a Starbucks barista calling to say that Jack's new worker didn't seem to know his communication program well enough to support him to have the usual conversation he and his colleagues looked forward to: "Is it alright if I just show him? I have a break coming up." And we began to learn…

10

Since our initial personal networks project, which was for four facilitators to support about 11 individuals, half of whom had no discernable network, we've gone on to develop curricula and workshop programs that we've delivered in communities from Nashville to Fort St John (just below the Alaska Highway) to nearly 4000 people; we've written articles and a book that constitutes a best-seller in our field; we've created a blog/e-newsletter that has got about 18,000 hits; we've organized days together for local experts in support networks of all kinds so that we could share our passion and problem-solve; we've hosted experts in this particular field of expertise of community support to big and small audiences; we've consulted and facilitated and led and followed and walked beside... and everywhere we go, people with disabilities and their family and friends – even the ones who haven't been happy and who we've been warned about – say, "This is what we wanted to talk about." And they give us hugs.

The most receptive and excited have been self-advocates. Why did we not see earlier that this conversation, focused on what many people with disabilities are, indeed, better at than most "regular" folks, would be a topic of interest? My old friend and mentor, the late Arnold Bennington, long-time People First board member, would be laughing at me. Again. And, like Arnold during his life, we have made an enviable lot of friends.

> **"You can learn new things at any time in your life if you're willing to be a beginner. If you actually learn to like being a beginner, the whole world opens up to you."**
>
> **Barbara Sher**

Our agency has changed significantly because of all of these interactions. What we offer has changed radically to become "supports we assist to organize" rather than services; what we look for in successful supports is different – did we get out of the way? Did we support friends and family and individuals to lead? Does the person have a champion?

We have been supported powerfully in all of this by all those who work at our agency, from our staff who are willing to look at new ways to do things, or who come to us from other places because they've been called to a mission and are seeking a setting where change is possible, to our colleagues who take on part of our work so that we can go do workshops. Jim, Susan, Ernie (our Executive Director) and I get to talk about what we do with supportive peers. Each conversation leads to another incremental shift, to, as Susan says, "making the implicit, explicit."

Constantly, we meet staff, managers, leaders and families who do not have this luxury and who are alone, wherever they live, trying to focus on these kinds of personal networks, often in isolation. In some places it's a single mom. In other agencies it's one worker going against the tide, and staying on because of his commitment to an individual. Sometimes they are surrounded by people who believe that everything else is more important than this. Is the paperwork done? Has the menu plan been changed? Has some form been ticked off. Often staff who are great relationship builders tell us that they've been criticised on evaluations for "fooling around" and "getting distracted," by, in fact, *connecting*. And yet they continue to do it, because they can see it's the most important thing to those they care about.

Margaret Wheatley says in an essay, "Are We All In This Together?", "We may even be waking up to the fact that most people want to help others, want to be generous, and care a great deal about the welfare of neighbors and strangers. We can rely on human goodness." There's a need for community – for those who want to support such networks to feel they are not alone, for them to have

12

permission – knowing that you are not alone is in itself a kind of permission to proceed, and then there's just the questions, "How do I do this? How do I show others how to do it? How do I lead? How do I increase the leverage of the idea that support networks are vitally important?" We've been lucky to have opportunities to ask these questions of those we meet, again and again: "How do you do that?" In this book we've tried to bring together some of what we've heard and tried for ourselves.

Our first book, *101 Ways to Make Friends: Ideas and Conversation Starters for People with Disabilities and Their Supporters*, was based on a collection of ideas from family, friends, neighbours and self-advocates, so it seemed like a simple thing to create a companion "how to" volume based on these conversations and on our own work as facilitators of groups of self-advocates (we freely admit this is our favourite part of this work.

One of the things I'm particularly grateful for is the encouragement of so many of my friends to make art again – my original degrees are in fine arts and printmaking, and then I got wonderfully "distracted" by my vocation . . . learning the PATH process with Linda Perry was my first return to paper and markers, and then, with Susan and Jule and my self-advocate

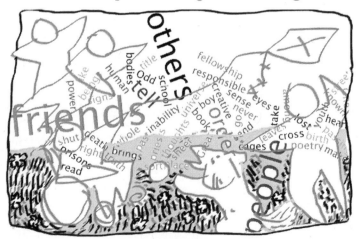

9 quotes from Virginia Woolf about friends, a wordle in a park

friends, the illustrations for a

13

few books.

Here is my funny art story. Making art is a scary, mostly lonely process and I had few regrets about moving into a world where I worked so often on teams I loved, with people I cared about. Soon after Linda showed me how to do the graphic illustrations for a PATH we did a tour of the north, helping people with planning as we went. On our first PATH I was standing nervously in front of this big huge white expanse of paper with a dozen people staring at me, waiting for me to draw their dreams for the focal person they cared about. But one doesn't hesitate with Linda. So off I went, increasingly lost in the dreams, the aspirations of fast-talking friends, the excitement, the visions of the grandparents and cousins and uncles and friends from school and the amazing veto power of the focal person who moved her eyes right for yes, and left for no. And if she moved her eyes left for "no" I then had to figure out how to turn the airplane I'd just drawn into something else – a Christmas tree perhaps.

> **"Tension is who you think you should be; relaxation is who you are."**
>
> *Chinese proverb*

As I drew I got lost in the vision and, on another level, in remembering art I loved – I started drawing figures from Monet, Hockney, turning the young woman in a wheelchair into a figure from a Van Eyck painting – turning the meadow someone dreamed she moved through into a kind of Jackson Pollack... it was like jazz music and I was at the top of my form. At the end, I was exhausted, sweating, incredibly satisfied, thinking "I was absolutely made for this." The young lady's grandfather came up and thanked me for co-facilitating, which was nice. "You've got guts," he said, "standing up here in front of all these people, drawing." He shook his head in disbelief. "I mean," he said, "I could see it if you could actually draw – but..." he kind of waved a the PATH, "y'know... we just appreciate that you could be here, and that you put the *effort* in." How lovely, eh? After all the insecurity of carting my portfolio around, talking to galleries, applying for exhibitions, winning an award or two while others didn't (or they did, and I didn't) – after all of that, here I am, doing my absolute best and being thanked for my *effort*. Somehow, *home.*

I think of what I do now as a kind of "community art" – self-advocates come up and say "I could have drawn that," and I think, "Yes, you could!" These drawings were done on the computer, using a Bamboo tablet and a couple of small drawings programs (SketchBookPro is my favourite), and they are looser and more interested in texture than meaning. I call them my palimpsest drawings as they are almost always layers over layers. I also need to give credit to www.wordle.net - which makes artistic word clouds out of text you enter.

The quotes are quotes that Susan, some friends and I started gathering some time ago – things to keep one going... pithy wisdom for self-pitying moments. Some times what we need are reminders that we're on course, and strong enough, and that everything will work out.

If we started to thank people, we'd forget someone. We've tried to mention by name those we've learned specific ideas from in each section. But a few people have supported us in exceptional ways – the consistently inspiring and idea-provoking Jule Hopkins from C.L.B.C.; Dr. Michael Kendrick, who has supported us to ask better questions; Dr. David Pitonyak, who keeps grounding us in what matters – who is in our lives and how we are made stronger and

15

more than we were; Pat Fratangelo, who makes it all make sense, and the folks at TASH who have put so much work into annually putting on the conference at which we've done our best learning and, more recently, some teaching.

Aaron

Original Introduction to 101 Ways to Make Friends, 1st Edition

Introduction

For more than twenty years, we have been involved in conversations with folks with disabilities and their supporters about relationships – feelings of loss, feelings of connection – "am I doing too much?" "am I not doing enough?" "is anyone else out there?" – fears and uncertainty that people with disabilities are not accepted as citizens in their communities. We've talked with parents of all ages who are planning for a future when their son or daughter will not have them to rely on (or refusing to plan because they can't bear to think about it) and with young people transitioning into a future in which they will be more independent and will need friends to rely on for practical and emotional reasons. But most of these talks have occurred "off the side of our desks" and within other planning contexts.

In 2007 we took on a demonstration project through Community Living British Columbia in which we examined the support

16

networks (family, friends, advocates, co-workers, neighbours) of eight people with disabilities. Part of the project was to look at ways to expand the networks of those who had involved friends and family and, for half of the people involved, who had no one they could depend on in their lives, to look at ways in which people with few or no unpaid relationships could be assisted to develop a network of supporters.

What we discovered quite soon was that many of the things we assumed were in place for everyone our agency supported were not actually happening. Ouch. People didn't have address books, they didn't have trusted facilitators or family members helping them negotiate the often fraught field of relationships, nor was there a plan to fill that gap. Things happened, or had happened, and no one really debriefed or processed events with them and allowed them to go on, wiser and more (or less) open to the next relationship. Instead, grief and confusion accrued. So we got a chance to figure out some of those things. Our Executive Director, Ernie Baatz, was supportive of the project throughout and said, "This is some of the most important learning we've done in 20 years."

Around the province three other groups worked on similar projects and what all of us discovered is that a) the support of unpaid relationships is an idea in its infancy – we might be doing a great job of supporting people in their communities and expanding our ideas of what folks' lives can look like, but we're just beginning to delve into the idea of natural relationships that are supported by systems; b) that unpaid relationships can be fostered and strengthened with very simple ideas that are easily put into place and conversations that are easy (and fun) to have; and perhaps most importantly, c) it is POSSIBLE for folks with disabilities to be and have great friends and supporters, even if they are currently isolated.

17

Later, we expanded the conversation and tried to find others who were also interested in these ideas, to build a network of mutually supportive friends, one person at a time. We've found that the hardest thing for people to hold on to in all of this is hopefulness. We met families who were doing incredible things with their family member with a disability, but felt they weren't doing enough. Folks with disabilities who worked hard on their networks, had taken all the classes, done all the homework, and still felt inadequate. A number of things became evident:

- The most important thing is to stay hopeful.
- Find ways to give leadership for their relationships to the folks we support.
- Identify clear, reasonable goals.
- Make a place for the conversations that need to happen.
- Don't assume anything.

So, on the one hand, where networks are happening in a conscious way, people are not feeling successful because they have rarely identified what success is and, instead, are thinking "we could be doing more." On the other hand, where it's not happening, people don't know how to proceed. So we started keeping this list of "things that are missing and easy to fix." An address book, for example. Life with an address book that works for you is completely different from life without an address book. One has ready, simple, self-directed access to connections - pick up your address book, find a friend, make a date to do something, build the relationship. Those moments - movies, going for coffee, an impromptu bowling afternoon or a walk through a park - are the building blocks that create the relationship that we depend on when we're ill or in distress or facing a decision that we're unsure about. No address book = no bowling date = no one to call when you're off to emergency or when you get bad news and the professional says "Is there someone I should call?" Likewise, setting a concrete goal:

"In the next three months I will take a cooking class and invite a fellow student to come to my house to practise a recipe." You can either succeed or you can be working on it, learning more about how to proceed to success but once you've got the goal you've got hope and, if you reach it, something to celebrate and build on. "I want friends" or "We want him to have friends" is a much harder thing to pin down and be successful with.

Different people, with and without disabilities, have different address books - some are written, some are on their computers, some are in the memories of their phones - but they have those numbers and can use them. We kept meeting folks with disabilities who had no address books. We'd talk to their staff teams and hear "well, they lost it," as if that explained why it didn't exist. We went back to the people who had address books and asked them if they ever lost them, and, heck, it turned out that we've all lost address books of various kinds and it doesn't mean we can yet do without one; what it means is that we need an "address book backup plan" – keeping everything on the computer and reprinting it, or having a second address book with important contacts written down in case the first one gets lost. We made an initial list of indicators of relationships, and "has an address book," was one of the items on the list. We predicted 80% of the folks would have address books, which was the reverse of what we found (80% did not).

This is an early stage in our research and experiences of this aspect of community living and we're looking forward to seeing and doing more and talking to more folks and their supporters; we've already begun to seize opportunities to travel and meet people and talk to them about their successes and challenges in this area. But, already, it has become apparent to us that these are conversations that many, many, many people need to have in all kinds of situations – individuals, communities, organizations where people gather, children, schools. And no one is more experienced or able

19

to show us the way than the people who are at the heart of this discussion, those who fought to close institutions and overcome age-old stereotypes to gain the right of citizenship. We often talk about how systems, not just structures, can become institutional – and how the language of community living continues to separate people by emphasizing differences instead of similarities (even referring to it as "community living" implies an alternative – institutional living – which remains a very real threat to people in other provinces and other parts of the world where institutions continue to thrive). The service system that has evolved over the past couple of decades has allowed people to be physically integrated, but many remain socially isolated, surrounded by paid staff and professionals in special classrooms or programs for groups of adults with disabilities. Funding and eligibility criteria drive the planning, not relationships. The very systems that were designed to include people continue to separate them from community; not having friends increases their risk of isolation.

Some of the best ideas in this book came from folks with disabilities who have built their own personal support networks, often without (or even despite) our assistance as paid supporters. The lessons to be learned from their example cannot be understated. The idea that people with developmental disabilities can not only live in community, but have valued and reciprocal relationships as friends and neighbours, represents a huge shift in thinking. As service providers, we must learn to facilitate, rather than supplant, these natural relationships – to expand our thinking about the gifts and contributions folks have to offer and be appreciated for.

The more we look at this issue of personal support networks, the more clear – and impassioned – we become about our mission as an agency. We're not just providing services...we're building community.

We hope that the work of so many people who have brought us to this pivotal point in our history means that institutions will never re-open and that large and "institutionalised" support systems will continue to downsize and personalise and that "community living" will not signify the threat of the alternative but will come to demonstrate the capacity for leadership that is in our field.

Susan Stanfield (Kurliak) and Aaron Johannes
Spectrum Society for Community Living (2009)

Some General Facilitation Tips

There are lots of great books on facilitation, and some wonderful teachers and classes. You can learn a lot by just being watchful when you get a chance to be with a really good facilitator. The other thing we've found is that good facilitators LOVE to talk about their work and don't get nearly enough opportunities to do so. As in our original project when folks we supported asked for deeper connections with those who might be friends, no leader that we have asked for assistance said "no" and in fact have said "yes" quite happily.

Here are some things we try to remember, in particular with people with disabilities but these tips work for all groups of people.

Look up the word "facilitate" – it means to "make easier." Our friend Linda Perry used to point out that this is a very different function than teaching, or telling, or arguing for change. Instead, we are there to listen, and then when we are certain of what that person, or that group, wants we make it easier if we can. This can

Hi

be a very relaxing idea for some people. For other people, it means there is no way to prepare. Yikes! They say. (Aaron is more of the first group.)

Go slow. Make sure that people are comfortable and that they are following what you're saying. In Aaron's avocation supporting People First groups of self-advocates to do presentations, one of the things he's learned is that

23

they want twice as many "breaks" to ask if everyone understand what's happening, and if anyone has questions, than most of us prepare for. Have a "check-in" attitude.

Make notes in big bold print about the ideas that are being discussed. Remember that everyone, including people with disabilities, learns in different modalities: listening, seeing, acting out scenarios, talking through ideas.

Have handouts that are clear and big enough for people to read and follow along.

Draw when you need to. Remember not everyone reads and, again, some people learn better from drawings. You don't need to be an expert artist. Part of the reason we have used new drawings instead of the more careful, clear ones from our first book was that we wanted to show how you can use messy scribbly drawings to explain things.

Sit everyone in a circle if you can; be impatient with places that look like classrooms. Speak to those furthest away and ask if they can hear you. Our least favourite moments have been reading feedback sheets that say "I couldn't hear anything from the back of the room," after 7 hours of talking.

Don't second-guess yourself in mid-thought. Don't argue with people. Don't work with a group so large that you can't connect with each of them by looking around the room and meeting their eyes. It's not a lecture; it's facilitation.

An important part of our first Personal Support Networks Project was the idea of "co-learning" – a pedagogical technique where the "instructor" assumes they will learn side by side with the "student." To reinforce this, we asked our first facilitators to keep journals of

24

how they found themselves changing, as well as notes on the folks they were supporting as part of our project.   Pay attention to your own learning.

Do have a "parking lot."   This is an idea that Barb Goode taught us – whatever people don't understand, put it up in the parking lot so you can make sure that when there is time it can be addressed. Or address it by asking if someone else can take on the job of clarifying... who knows what might come out of that connection? Barb also uses a list of words that people don't understand – a kind of working glossary that you can make as words come up.

If there's limited time, give out sticky notes or "dot" stickers – write down what most people want to talk about, and then have people vote with three dots each for their 1st, 2nd and 3rd choices – be impatient with those who try to do it all.   Meaghan Feduck calls this kind of choice-making a "dot-mocracy" – it also gives people a chance to move around a bit and it's fun.

Get some feedback, all through the workshop, but certainly by the end of the day you want to have an idea of how things went. Facilitation is very tiring sometimes, and can be quite dis-couraging... you want to know that your day was worth-while.

Don't expect all raves – some people might not have a great day. Assume that 10% of them are in the wrong place at the wrong time, which is the general percentage of people in any given site who should probably be elsewhere.   But also don't attribute or project things on to people, ever.   Some of the most shocking feedback has been from people who we thought were glaring at us, hating us, hating everything we stood for – and then at the end of the day they handed us back a feedback sheet that says something like, "I came in here ready to quit – I only came because it meant I didn't have to go to work – but the truth is I love my actual job with the folks I support but didn't know how to do what I wanted to / needed to do with and for them.   Now I do.   Thanks for giving me my joy back."

Seriously.   It happens more than you would think.

Celebrate

Here's another story – we ended up invited into a long-term care hospital and we talked about what we talk about – people in unpaid, committed, reciprocal relationships – and the staff, all of them in uniforms, sat there with their arms crossed sneering at us the whole time.   Some of them asked challenging questions – not hard questions, but questions poised to trip us up.   It was a scary group... and yet you could also see that they really cared about the people they were supporting, deeply.   They just didn't believe in our approach.   What we suggested was, not least, risky.   A year later the Social Worker called us up and said, "Well you completely changed their lives – they'd never had anyone tell them those things before but after a week or so they realized that they could get off the ward, that the people they cared about had something to offer others, that there was a whole world out here waiting for them!"   In a year, some had got jobs, some had gone on holidays, some had reconnected with family, all of them had significantly better lives. "And the staff are happier too!" he said.   This isn't meant to be bragging – we didn't do the work, we didn't challenge ourselves to change, we didn't hold ourselves accountable in a whole new way: they did.

Our friend David says, "You never know what's going to come out of a single conversation – it might be incredible."

26

Which leads to the last idea here, which is that we can't facilitate one kind of approach with those we support, and another with team members. If we are going to say that one group, those we support, should be open and honest and focused on relationships, we need to look at be vigilant in how we treat staff and volunteers in our agencies and in our homes.

Check out the resources section for some good books, videos and websites that will be useful if you want to be a better facilitator.

Say hello to the next person you see (1)

There is a remarkable difference, once you start noticing how people interact, between those who naturally say "Hello" as they walk up to people they don't yet know, and those who hang back.

Many years back, when we first began teaching "social skills" to small groups of self-advocates, we realized that the staff who were there to support them often had less practise in making connections than the folks in the learning group. And support staff have been equally excited about learning and practising new skills. One young fellow came up and told us that "I did everything you said, and I met someone and we got married. Thanks." That was fun!

In our workshops when we look at this initial way for folks to make friends we get people to say "hello" to each other and, sometimes, we talk about how it feels and that this is the first step – a greeting that makes it easier the next time we see that person to more naturally say hello; this first hello might lead to a whole future relationship. Apparently it could lead to marriage!

Sometimes we get people to say hello to the person sitting next to them, sometimes we get them to choose someone they've never met before and say hello, and (if the session allows enough time) interview them and then introduce them to the rest of the group.

Our friend and colleague Joanne, one of our facilitators in our initial project, decided to experiment in a new neighbourhood where she didn't yet know anyone.

> "When you are kind to others, it not only changes you, it changes the world."
>
> **Harold Kushner**

In her old neighbourhood everyone talked to each other and there was a friendly feeling. She missed that. Here, in a new diverse neighbourhood, no one knew each other or even shared the same language. She was walking her dog and she had been teaching staff and folks with disabilities to greet possible new friends. She decided that she'd be brave herself and just start with one hello to one person. She said hello to the next person; they didn't look up to say hello back. She kept trying and every time she and her dog passed a new person, she greeted them. Soon people were saying hello back, or smiling and nodding to her and her dog. Within a few months people were saying hello when they saw her coming, and trying to tell her things about their gardens, their own pets, their children, their grandchildren, their lives.

Wise

She says that a few months later she looked out the window and saw two neighbours stopping on the street to chat, a thing she'd never seen before. She realized it was true: one person can make a difference.

One person, one dog, taking one step together towards a friendly neighbourhood and making a difference! A good first lesson in our work facilitating relationships.

Questions to ask: How do *you* say hello?

- What's the most natural way for you to greet people? Do you shake hands? Smile? Wave?

- What might happen after you say "Hello?" within five minutes? Five days? Five weeks? Five years?

Things to do:

- Role play saying hello to a new person.

Try your own version of a "hello" experiment like Joanne's:

I will say hello to people when my dog and I pass them, no matter what. *Or,*

I will say hello to people on the bus. *Or,*

I will say hello to everyone in the coffee shop when I go there in the mornings.

Make eye contact; smile (2)

Things to talk about:

For some folks with disabilities and for some people from other cultures, making eye contact is hard, yet it's a great initial way of connecting with people and, like saying "hello" it is one of the first ways that we notice who might want to be our friend – because they are intent on meeting our gaze.

Cat X 4

Questions to discuss:

- How do you make eye contact with a stranger?

- Do you know anyone with a disability who doesn't "talk" but has a different way of communicating? Do they use their eyes to say what they mean?

Things to practise:

- Role play making eye contact with someone new. Try having people communicate with their eyes. We have some great friends who communicate in ways that are not usual – we should all have a sense of what that's like. If there are support staff or parents, encourage them to try it too.

- Reinforce the "rules" of the group if you're supporting more than one person – focus on "positive and possible" and no teasing or making people feel bad: this is an opportunity in a safe place to learn from each other. Give gentle feedback, be positive.

- Role play, showing with your eyes, that you're interested in

> **"The world's definitions are one thing and the life one actually lives is quite another. One cannot allow oneself, nor can one's family, friends, or loves – to say nothing of one's children – to live according to the world's definitions: one must find a way, perpetually, to be stronger and better than that."**
>
> **James Baldwin**

knowing more about this new person.

- o What about if you *don't* want to know this person: if you don't feel safe in the neighbourhood or with someone who is trying to talk to you – what happens with your eyes then?

Tell people you want to make friends (3)

Things to talk about:

Our friend Michael who teaches us a lot always says "Nothing is better without planning." Planning to increase or deepen someone's network begins by figuring out who is already there for them: friends, professionals, family members and other supports. Like finding a new job or a new place to volunteer, the best way to increase your chances of success are to talk to people you already know about what you might like to do and see what ideas they have. They may have been thinking for years that they should introduce you to another of their friends and this will give them an opening to do this.

Questions to discuss:

Have you ever had a meeting, or part of a meeting, where friendship was the topic? What was that like?

Everyone needs help sometimes. How do we ask for what we need? Is it hard? Are there ways to make it easier?

Who do you think might help you make friends? Are there people within the support network who make friends easily? If you were arriving in a new place and didn't know anyone, and wanted some help getting connected, where would you go?

Things to practise:

Practise asking someone for help with making friends.

Things to try

Try making up some role playing cards and divide people up into pairs and have them take turns asking each other for help. Here are some you can photocopy and cut up. There are two blank cards for other ideas that the group might have. It can also be fun, with a group that meets regularly, to get them to generate the ideas for the cards and then deal them out so that people don't get their own idea to role play.

I have a lot of people in my life but what I'd like is to get closer to some of those people. Could you help me do that?	When I go to church I see people talking afterwards. There's also a coffee club, but I'm too shy to go. Would you help me to get more involved?	Sometimes people seem friendly and seem to like me, but I want to know how I can tell who my friends really are. Can you help me do that?	I want to have a meeting of everyone in my life and talk to them about being my circle of support. Could you help me do that?
Sometimes I worry about what I would do if there was an emergency. I have some people in my life but I'm not sure if I could call on them. I don't know what to do.	I need help figuring out who I know and who I can trust. Do you have any ideas?		

35

Make a list of everyone you know (4)

It was a big surprise for everyone close to our friend Gary when we got together and each of us made a list of who was in his life; while there was some overlap, they were very different lists! And the newest people in his life had noticed things that those of us who had known him longer hadn't even noticed, or had stopped noticing. There are lots of ways to figure out who you know and how they fit into your life. You can make a list of people that you know and split it into people who are friends, people who are acquaintances, people you know just to wave to. You can circle the people you really trust and you can put stars besides the people that you'd like to get to know better.

A common and useful tool is "circles," developed by the folks from Inclusion Press (see "resources" for the website and support this amazing Canadian resource known all over the world – one of our under-appreciated national treasures). Photocopy the "circles" on the facing page and get people to fill it out. If you find it useful, check out www.inclusion.com for a DVD of great tools and the rights to use them.

Things to talk about:

The often-asked question is: can a staff be a friend? Two experts we admire come from absolutely opposite sides on this one. One says absolutely not, the other one says absolutely - they *must* be... and we have heard everyone else in between. We don't believe in taking sides about anything except human rights and kindness.

> "Feeling unworthy is like putting a huge obstacle into the God force, into the life force which is everywhere."
>
> **Dr. Wayne Dyer**

But we do believe in thinking critically about the roles of everyone in the lives of folks with disabilities. And what we have found is that not only have folks not had any opportunity to think this through, with some help, but also that their staff have rarely been given opportunities to talk about this.

In fact, staff are often very confused by the mixed messages we've given them and the lack of discussion of their *feelings* – one new Executive Director will tell them they should give in to their impulse to be friends; but a Social Worker might tell people that if they need friends with disabilities, there must be something wrong with them; one manager will say they need to maintain a professional distance, the next will say that they should and can be friends – but then they'll be transferred from one "program" to another, without a thought about the person they have come to care about. Staff need opportunities to talk about this issue and they need clarity from those who support them.

There are some important things to consider. Can each staff be a friend to everyone? What will their role be when they are no longer paid to be there? Has anyone you know been in the position of losing favourite staff, and if so, what has been the outcome?

Many folks with disabilities have been provided with services that don't focus on helping them to learn who their friends are or who they can trust. Folks often need opportunities to talk about the difference, and then more opportunities to talk about who will really be there for them when needed, because they might well have great friends who are unable to support them in situations that require more assertiveness or better understanding of things like how the medical system or the justice system works.

Questions to discuss:

What's the difference between a friend, an acquaintance, and

37

someone who is in your intimate circle? Who would go with you to the Doctor if you needed help? If you won a lottery, who would you most want to celebrate with? Who could you trust to help you figure out what to do next?

Things to practise:

Try making a list for someone, or get folks to work on their own lists. If there are enough participants helping folks with disabilities we ask them to do their own lists or "circles" first – to look at their own networks of support and relationships and reflect over the vulnerability that this exercise can arouse in people. Often staff will report that "I don't have a life" or "I really need some closer friends." It's okay to know this – it's where you are, and you can't get to where you want to be without knowing where you are. Now you just need a plan...

...and a plan for the person you support!

Things to try

If there are enough people with circles filled out, ask some theoretical questions:

- If John wanted more friends, could he share part of Mary's circle?

- If Mary needed more support around something in her outer circle, could she "borrow" that from John? Could he help her

"Each has his past shut in him like the leaves of a book known to him by his heart, and his friends can only read the title."

Virginia Woolf

find a good Doctor or develop a relationship with the local librarian?

Actions I want to take

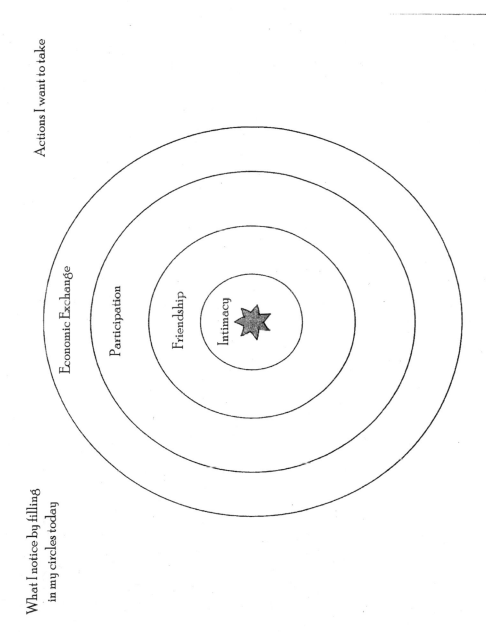

Economic Exchange

Participation

Friendship

Intimacy

What I notice by filling
in my circles today

41

Walk into anything an equal, with much to be proud of (5)

Everyone has gifts and strengths, no matter their level of genius or their challenges. In this conversation – how to develop a network of supports – it's important to reinforce this idea.

For instance, folks with disabilities often know more about developing friendships and fostering relationships than folks who have not had to rely so much on others.

Things to talk about:

Having emotional and social needs met is more important than almost any other factor in the creation of a successful life.

Conversations about equality can bring up many different emotions and can expose people's vulnerabilities, so be prepared to support folks through this.

Gamble Everything

Questions to discuss:

What are your gifts? What are some things that people regularly compliment you on? Write these qualities down as a list.

What makes you feel like an equal? Who listens to you and makes you feel like what you are saying is important?

Who makes you feel unequal? What kinds of situations make you feel less than equal?

Things to practise:

Depending on the group, you can try different things.

Thinking about your answers to the above questions about equality, role play making others feel equal.

Split into threes and practise "listening like it matters." One person talks, the other is "a good listener" and the third watches and gives feedback.

It's also fun, with a group that has a lot of confidence and is fun-loving, to try the same exercise but with one participant being "a bad listener."

Things to try

In between now and your next meeting, when you feel someone is really listening to you and paying attention and treating you well, tell them how much you appreciate it. Everyone in the support network should try this.

Self-advocates often tell us that the best listeners they have in their lives are their pets.

Notice whether telling people how much you appreciate their attentiveness helps them (or you) to be better listeners.

When people listen attentively to you, does it increase your feeling of equality?

Use affirmations (6)

Think of affirmations as positive self-talk. When folks start thinking negatively, it is easy for them to get caught up in a subconscious and repetitive script of negativity.

By thinking positively we can change the pattern, but we need to practise. Repetition is crucial. We need to bombard our sub-conscious with positive thoughts constantly in order to replace the negative ones.

Things to talk about:

The more negative the people around us are, the easier it is for us to fall into negative thought patterns. The whole support network needs to be involved for affirmations to replace negative thinking. If we are all working on becoming more positive, the welcome side-effect is that we all learn to focus on our own gifts and strengths.

Questions to discuss:

> **"No road is long with good company."**
>
> **Turkish Proverb**

Are there ways to make the environment of the person being supported more positive?

Are there specific negative thoughts that individuals could focus on turning around into positive thoughts?

How can folks make sure to have several opportunities to repeat affirmations each day?

Things to practise:

Write down your affirmations on post-its and leave them around where you are sure to see them. Don't forget to add your list of gifts and strengths from the previous section "Walk into anything an equal, with much to be proud of."

If reading is a challenge, would drawings or photos work better than reminder notes? Our friend Adam starts off every day with a picture of himself that lists all his gifts. Making audio and video recordings of your affirmations can be helpful too.

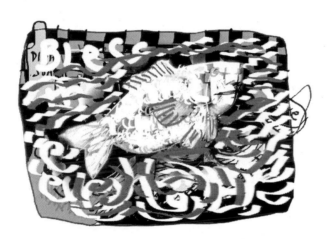

Kitchen Sink Blessing

Things to try

Use the Affirmation Worksheet on the next page to come up with a list of "I am" and "I can be" statements. "I am" is about who you are right now. "I can be" is about what your aspirations are for your future.

For example "I am a good listener" and "I can be a great listener."

This worksheet has been adopted from many "mainstream" examples, but mostly from the work of Jack Canfield. Initially we felt a little funny about simplifying something like this – we're not psychologists or even personal coaches – but after using it with some groups and getting amazing feedback not just from people

45

with disabilities but from their supporters, we're more convinced. One mom came up to us at the end of a workshop saying, "I have been to so many self-development workshops and have read so many books about this, and I've never been able to think of a single positive thing about myself, so I just felt worse. I used this form just to keep my daughter company and now look – " and she showed us a whole sheet of things about herself that she was able to identify as positive qualities. She was so excited.

An affirmation is a short "I statement"

The reason for affirmations is to replace the negative self-talk that we all have in our heads, about how we can't do something or we're worried or...

I am: A statement of who you are.

I am strong
I am enthusiastic
I am relaxed

or you can make an "I can" statement:

I can: A statement of your potential.

You can accomplish goals. You have accomplished some already. Make a statement of your belief in your power to grow, to change, and to help yourself.   You might want to say:

I can get a job
I can sing
I can learn to cook rice pudding

The most important thing is to use your affirmations all the time, to put them in places where you'll see them, and where they'll surprise you (on your mirror, in your wallet, inside your drawer, on your toaster) so that they help you replace the negative statements in your brain with positive ones.

" I am _____."

"I can _____."

Make a community inventory (7)

A community inventory is like a map of the opportunities in your neighbourhood for building your personal network. Have people take note of the places they might like to visit; places where they think they might be comfortable. Have them notice, as well, of the people in their neighbourhood. Maybe someone they would like to get to know better is already a regular in one of the places in their community.

Map

Things to talk about:

Discuss what is in your neighbourhood. Also, who is in your neighbourhood? Pay special attention to the clubs, community centres, churches, or recreation facilities near you, and make a list. Any good stores, restaurants or coffee shops should be on your list. Are there places to work? Meet up with old friends? Meet new friends? Volunteer?

Questions to discuss:

What is it like going to a new place? How does your community feel about different cultures? How do you feel? A lot of people are

48

comforted by having something of their own culture in their neighbourhood. Is there someplace in your community that connects you to your culture?

Things to practise:

Go for a walk and make list of what is on each block. Pick out a few places you might like to try.

Things to try:

Try going into one of the new places. If that works out, great! If not, keep trying new places at a pace that is not stressful for you. When you find somewhere you like, make a plan to go regularly – same time/same place. After you have found one place you like, think about whether there are any other places you'd like to try.

Find out what's special about your city or neighbourhood (8)

Debra loved our local Trout Lake Luminaries Festival so much that she lived right beside it, and she wanted to be involved. Different years she did different things, but what she really wanted was to be one of the fire jugglers. Step by step, she finally learned how to walk to juggle fire. Another friend, who has a disability and didn't want to juggle fire, volunteered to hand out brochures. Both these people had a great time and got invited to the big volunteers' party afterward.

Things to talk about:

Every city or neighbourhood has special events like festivals, cultural events, concerts, block parties; the list is endless. How might people research their options? Local newspapers are one great resource – what are some others?

There is something for everyone, and there are always ways to get involved.

Questions to discuss:

What are your passions? Are there festivals, concerts, sports or other activities that especially interest you?

If you are an animal lover, are there shelters nearby that need volunteers? Is there a 4h Club or an Aquarium Society? A leash-free dog park?

In what ways would you like to get involved, and who do you need to talk to about participating?

Things to practise:

Role play how you might approach a group to volunteer your time. Think in terms of your strengths and your gifts. Remember that you have plenty to offer, and that groups are always looking for new volunteers.

Things to try:

Bring in copies of the local newspaper to find out what is happening that people might want to take part in. Don't forget to check out the smaller neighbourhood newspapers too.

Go into your local community centre or church and see if they have a newsletter. Many businesses have bulletin boards loaded with current activities. Ask around about what is special about your neighbourhood and how you could participate.

Become a "regular" (9)

Aaron noticed that when he went out with a friend of his, who has a disability, to the fellow's favourite coffee shop, all the staff knew his friend and had memorized his order, and many of the regulars said hello and asked how he was doing.

Having gone to his own local coffee shop every single morning for almost four years, Aaron couldn't help but compare his experience with his. None of the staff at his regular place knew his name or his drink, and no one ever said hi, let alone showed any interest.

He discussed this phenomenon with the manager of his coffee shop... who didn't really care. And now he is going to a new coffee shop, where they know what he likes and are excited to see him come through the door. Take a look at where you're spending your time and money.

One point of this story is that people with disabilities can be better at social interaction than the people in their personal networks. It is important for us to work on our own social skills in order to be able to give our best support to someone else. Another point is that if your current place is not working out for you, try a new place.

Things to talk about:

Going the same place at the same time each week, we start to recognize staff and other regulars, some of whom we might want to get to know better.

This might be a good time to talk about safety issues. Are there places you should avoid? Are their people you should not approach? What is okay to talk about? What is not? Gauge your group and decide what needs talking about. Often people with disabilities have been trained not to talk to strangers, but not how to meet new friends, and want to talk about that.

Questions to discuss:

Where are the good places in your neighbourhood to be a regular? Let people in your support network know if you are already a regular somewhere.

If you are a regular somewhere, are there already connections in place? Do you have an easy way to communicate with potential friends? If not, this is something you should work on.

Things to practise:

Walk around your neighbourhood and take note of the different restaurants, coffee shops and other meeting places. Pick some places where you think you will be comfortable.

Pick one place and think about what you will do when you first go in and what you will say to the people you meet.

> "It is our job as leaders not to succumb to this addiction to simplicity."
>
> **Dan Pallotta**

Things to try:

Now go into the place you have chosen. Notice whether any of the other patrons has something in common with you. For example, do they read the same newspaper as you do? Are they interested in sports? Do they order the same drink as you?

Start going to your chosen spot on the same day and at the same time each week. By doing so, you will begin to recognize other regulars.

Use the greeting you have practiced with one of the people you see regularly. If you are feeling brave, try starting a conversation about whatever it is you have in common.

Take part in a run for charity (10)

Being involved in a run for charity is a great way to meet people, not to mention that it feels good to be doing something positive for your community, and you are getting out into the fresh air!

If people in your facilitation group are not runners, they can sign up to cheer, pass out water, or work at the registration table. They will find that the same people keep showing up. There are often volunteer parties after the race and free t-shirts for those who help out.

Things to talk about:

Special Olympics has come up in this portion of almost every one of our workshops – and there are plenty of opportunities to be involved in sports or to volunteer your time in a variety of different roles within this fine organization.

Most places have runs throughout the year supporting various charities. If you try being involved in one charity run and you enjoy it, sign up for more!

Questions to discuss:

If you will be involved in the run itself, are you in shape? What do you need to do to get into shape? Many places put on training sessions and practice runs that can be really great places to meet people because they happen over a period of time.

Do you know anyone who is already a charity run volunteer, or someone else who might want to participate in it with you? Having an experienced partner might make things easier, especially the first time you give it a try.

Things to practise:

Get a map of the course. Even if you are walking or rolling, take a practice trip along the route.

If you are participating in other ways, such as handing out water, practice what you might say to people. Practice cheering!

Things to try:

Sign up to run or to volunteer for an upcoming charity run. When you are signing up, ask whether there are any orientation sessions you could take part in.

Host a games night (11)

Almost everyone loves playing a game of some kind. Game lovers usually have an assortment to choose from. Have people make a list of games they enjoy and then compare lists to see if anyone has similar interests.   You can even do this on Facebook and say something like "I want to play Cribbage – anyone want to join me?"

Things to talk about:

If you are the type of person who has a variety of games to pick from, you are sure to have some that everyone will enjoy.

People love to do things like this, but often no one thinks to be the host. Be the person in your group that brings people together!

Nothing says friendship like sharing good food. Make sure you have enough snacks and drinks for everyone. Don't be shy to ask your guests to bring along some of their favourite goodies.

It might be a good idea at this point to talk about what it means to be a 'good loser'. Games should be fun, and nothing will keep people away from your games night more than a host who can't stand to lose.

angels

Questions to discuss:

What games do you have? Are there other games that you would like to have? Think about asking the people you invite to bring along their favourite games.

Things to practise:

Practice playing your different games. Learn the rules so that you can teach your guests how to play. Role play how you might greet people when they arrive. Focus on fun!

Things to try:

Make your games night a regular activity. If you like, switch the games around each time. Be open to someone else hosting. Alternately, pick one or a few games that you know everyone likes, and stick with them. Try your hardest to make your games night as fun as possible for all of your guests!

Respect differences (12)

What we're trying to do is promote inclusion – so don't exclude any groups. Respect different cultures and sexual orientations. Think about what it feels like to be excluded because of our differences. Again, this will often be the first time folks with disabilities have had a chance to talk about this, unfortunately.

Things to talk about:

Depending on the group, you might want to discuss how, often, people from minority groups have had little opportunity to discuss what it is like to be from outside the majority culture.

Invite people to talk about their own experiences with prejudice.

Discuss how to overcome our prejudices. Remember, prejudice literally means to negatively pre-judge someone. In other words, we form pre-conceived ideas with no evidence to back them up.

Once we learn to get to know people on an individual basis, and once we make an effort to learn more about different cultures, countries and sexual orientations, we come to see that strangers are nowhere near as strange as we may have thought.

It's easy; base your choice of friends on the person, not on the group.

Questions to discuss:

What is it like to be from outside the majority group? People of different cultures, or religions, or gay and lesbian folks, often feel loneliness and isolation. What can we do to make everyone feel welcome?

Are there folks in your network who are from more than one minority group? How does that feel?

Things to practise:

Go out of your way to be friendly towards people of different cultures, religions or sexual orientations. Role play greeting people from outside of your usual circle.

56

Things to try:

Go to a different church. Try out restaurants and cafes in your neighbourhood that are from outside of your own culture. Attend your local Gay Pride Parade. Attend events put on by minority cultures. If you are in a city that's large enough, call the local gay and lesbian association and ask if they have someone who can come talk to your group. In Boston, a terrific woman named Pauline is starting groups for gay, lesbian, transgender, bi and questioning people – she's started four groups already and is finding lots of people who have lots of questions!

TIP: Google 'my town' cultural events, or ask about upcoming cultural events at your local community centre.

Walk or take transit as much as you can (13)

We think of public transit as the great equalizer. Nobody ever made a new friend being driven around in a van.

Transportation is one of the top three things that people talk about, which they feel holds them back from doing what they want to be doing. The other two are money and fear.

By promoting transit, we are demonstrating, teaching and supporting independence, and promoting equality and the possibility of connection.

Things to talk about:

Many folks with disabilities will never be able to drive. Public transit provides equal access for everyone. Talk about how it feels for one person to always be the driver and others to always be the passenger.

Questions to discuss:

57

Is accessibility an issue? If so, does your community have a HandyDart service for folks with mobility issues?

Things to practise: Many folks with disabilities are already experts at public transit. Ask one of those experts to help you prepare. Our friend Penny connects people with disabilities who are new to town with people who know their way around so that they can teach them the transit routes. Often this leads to

> **"Your time is limited, don't waste it living someone else's life. . . . Don't let the noise of other's opinion drown your own inner voice. And most important, have the courage to follow your heart and intuition, they somehow already know what you truly want to become. Everything else is secondary."**
>
> **Steve Jobs**

relationships as well as more independence. Most often, people are grateful to be asked, so don't be shy.

Things to try:

Once you have gotten through your initial trip, make a plan to take transit on a regular basis – again, aim to arrive the same stop at the same time. Are there people you know who are going the same way?

You will notice other people taking the bus at the same time as you do, so why not start saying hello to those folks?

TIP – If access to appropriate transit is a problem, have folks think about applying to sit on the board of their local transit authority. Many self-advocates have done this, and have championed improvements that make public transit easier to use for all folks with disabilities.

If you're shy or need help – find a leader for your own "friends" project (14)

The main thing that keeps folks from expanding their personal support networks is fear of the unknown. One way to deal with this nervousness is to have folks ask someone they trust to help them lead their "friends" project. Even some of the most capable, well-known self-advocates find this useful. It could be staff or family, or perhaps another self-advocate who has successfully built their own support network. *Remember, many folks with disabilities are real experts at social networking.*

Things to talk about:

Having someone to support you in growing your network is often a simple matter of asking someone to help you make goals. You'll find that people are glad to help and gratified to be included in process of expanding your network of friends.

Discuss the level of assistance necessary, as well as when to fade your support. Remember, once folks get over their initial shyness, they can often begin to take back the leadership of their own projects.

Questions to discuss:

What are the fears? Talking about their fears often helps people to understand them and to begin to get over them.

What kind of leadership do you need? Who is the best person to ask for help? Is there more than one person you can go to for support?

Things to practise: Role play asking a trusted person to help you

59

lead your "friends" project.

Chicken Music

Pick some easy first steps from *101 Ways to Make Friends* and try them out with the person you have chosen to help you.

Things to try: Make a list of the things you need help with, and revise the list as necessary. Talk with your chosen project leader often about how the process is working out for you.

Still feeling shy? Start with something small (15)

People often believe they are shy in social situations, but the reality may be that it is just plain scary going into unknown places where anything could happen.

Every journey begins with a single step. Starting with something smaller is a great way for people to build their confidence while taking positive steps toward their ultimate goal.

Things to talk about:

It is easy to become overwhelmed in social situations, even when we think we are prepared. It is always a good idea to go into such situations with a "plan b." If saying hi to the first person you see makes you nervous, how about starting with a friendly wave?

Questions to discuss:

If you feel too shy about any of the ways to make friends that we've gone over so far, are there portions of them that you could start with? How can you be involved in your goal of making new friends in a way that makes it easier for you to get started?

Things to practise:

Within your group, break down larger goals into their smaller parts, and choose one of those to start off with. For example, the goal of asking someone to dance at an upcoming night out might be too overwhelming, whereas if you were to begin with the goal of just making eye contact with someone, it could be more achievable, and it is a measurable step in the direction of your goal.

Alternately, for each goal, brainstorm a list of less stressful activities you could do to help you build up your courage. Using the dance example, perhaps the whole idea of focusing on meeting someone there makes you nervous. Your list of less stressful activities might include taking tickets at the door, or helping to serve drinks. Chances are that if you are at the dance serving drinks, you will start to feel more comfortable about meeting people there, many of whom you will find are just as timid as you are.

Our friend Mary was really anxious because she had never been to a dance before, but she really wanted to go to a high school dance – she'd seen so many in movies. Her teacher organized a job for her taking tickets at the door, but halfway through the night she had gotten over her inhibitions, and was dancing up a storm! The next time there was a dance, she was first in line to buy a ticket, she convinced all her girlfriends to come too, and there was no way she was standing behind the pop counter!

One more thing here: don't forget to keep practicing your

affirmations.

Things to try:

Take one smaller portion of your goal from the list you have made and rehearse it. If making eye contact at a dance is what you have chosen, practice making eye contact with the people in your network.

If taking tickets at the dance is one of the less stressful activities you have come up with, practice what you will say to people as they come in.

> "The wrong answer is the right answer in search of a different question."
>
> Bruce Mau

TIP – By now, people in your group have probably come up with some of their own ideas for building personal networks. Remind them to save their suggestions until you get to number 101!

16. Decide to accept the next invitation that comes your way

Openness is a great way to discover new skills and pleasures. Remind folks that if they are being invited to do something, the person who invited them is interested in *them.* They are opening themselves up for friendship.

Things to talk about:

Sometimes we get into the habit of turning down invitations. We can be nervous about trying new things or meeting new people. Again, keep in mind that invitations only come from people who are interested in us.

Just making the decision to be more open to invitations in general puts you in a position where things are bound to change for the positive.

Add this to your list of affirmations: "I am a person who gets invitations to participate."

By accepting invitations you are bound to find a bunch of new things that you like to do, but you may also find some things you don't like. That is okay too. In the process, we learn more about ourselves.

Questions to discuss:

How might things change for you if you become the type of person who is open to accepting invitations?

Can you remember any invitations you turned down and later wished that you had accepted? What would you do if someone invited you to go to a wrestling match? What if someone invited you to go to an art gallery? What if they invited you to go on a cruise with them? Aaron recently got invited to go to a WWE Wrestling event and to his surprise had an amazing time *and* made a new friend – someone who was with another friend and knew all about wrestling.

This is another opportunity to discuss safety. What kinds of invitations are safe to accept? Which are not safe?

Things to practise:

Rehearse accepting invitations. Have people change roles; take turns being the inviter and the invitee.

You might want to practice what you should do in the case of unsafe or unwanted invitations.

Things to try:

Be open to trying something you think you might not like. Be open to accepting invitations from people of other cultures or backgrounds. Consider making an agreement with everyone: we will all accept the next (safe) invitation that comes by.

Rehearse what you want to say ahead of time (17)

New social situations can leave anyone anxious and tongue-tied. People with disabilities (and others) need concrete examples in the form of rehearsed conversation starters to help them relax. By having folks talk about who will be there, and by practising ahead of time what they will say in social situations, their fears will subside. This works just as well for things like doctors appointments.

Remember to keep it all positive and hopeful. Don't say, "When you get there, don't hit yourself." Say something like, "When you get there, you are going to have a great time. You can stay as long as you like and leave whenever you are ready."

After the event, talk about what went well. Also talk about what you might do differently next time

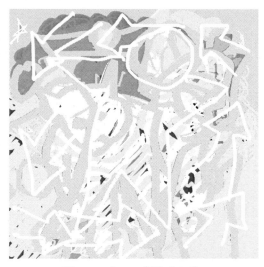

Memories of Friends

Things to talk about:

Pick one of the *101 Ways to Make Friends* that you want to try. Once you have picked one, discuss what the social component will be.

For example, if you have decided to start a conversation with someone you have noticed at your coffee shop, you might want to talk about what kind of a conversation you want to have. Think about what you might have in common with the person and then rehearse your introduction.

Talk about rejection, remembering to keep this conversation positive too. The fact is that what we perceive as rejection most often has nothing to do with us. Some people don't want new friends. Perhaps the person who seems to be rejecting us is dealing with some problem of their own and they simply don't have the energy or the space for a new relationship at the moment.

Questions to discuss:

What is it that makes you nervous about making new friends? How will rehearsing help you to lower your anxiety? What will you do when things go really well? How will you react if the person you have chosen to befriend is not interested?

Things to try:

Try rehearsing right before the activity. Using the coffee shop example, even though you have rehearsed often at home, it still helps to stop just outside the coffee shop and run through your rehearsal one more time. Then it is fresh in your mind.

TIP: Most people who are excellent at social interactions will tell you that there are two important things you need to learn. First, the hardest part of any new relationship, by far, is that very first interaction. And second, if someone does not want to be friends, do not blame yourself.

Have an address book that works for you (18)

In a recent survey of support networks for people with disabilities, our prediction was that 80 percent of the folks involved would have address books. The sad truth is that only 20 percent did.

Things to talk about:

As facilitators, we often use TV programs like 'CSI' as an example. Think about 'CSI' – what do the investigators look for when they are searching for a missing person? Think in terms of relationships and generate a list of those things.

If the investigators came into your house, would they be able to track you down? Do you have an accessible address book? Do you have a calendar of upcoming events? Is there any useful information on your fridge door? What about your personal mail, or your computer?

Questions to discuss:

What different kinds of address books are there?

What kind would be easiest for you to use?

Is one copy enough? How would you feel if you lost your only address book?

Things to practise:

Photocopy the contacts page (the last page) from '101 Ways to Make Friends', or bring address books with you and hand them out at the meeting you are facilitating. Then get folks to ask someone in their group for a phone

"There is more dignity in one thousand mistakes than one easy answer. There is more hope in a wrong choice freely selected than the right one provided by someone else"

Ari Ne'eman

number right now.

Look back at your circles exercise from the 4th way to make friends 'Make a List of Everyone You Know' and decide who needs to be in your address book.

Remember to include important people from your outside circles, such as your doctor, your dentist, and folks who you think you might want to move into your inner circles.

Things to try:

Go out and buy two address books. Carefully choose address books that will work for you. Have one to carry with you and another one to leave at home.

If you are into technology, you could alternately use a contacts program on your computer for at home, and your cell phone contacts application as your portable address book.

Whenever you get home with new contacts, don't forget to add them right away to your 'at home' address book.

TIPS:

Even if you are a whiz with technology, it is a really good idea to keep an old-fashioned paper address book around in case of emergencies like power outages or computer crashes.

Always keep your alternate address book in a different location than your day-to-day address book. Put it somewhere safe. You wouldn't want to lose both.

Make a relationship journal about each of your friends (add a blank journal page after this for facilitators to photocopy) 19

This is another idea that came from Joanne and her team.   Make

67

photocopies of the journal sheet on the next page and hand them out. Have folks write down one person they know, how they know them, what they usually do together, their contact information, any updates – then when they get home, they can put it into a binder called "My Network".

At home they can keep adding the pages to their "My Network" binder. Put them in alphabetical order, so that your friends are easy to find. Ours is just a suggested format; feel free to make changes for your group, but the idea is that the relationship journal could become not just a way to track relationships, but allow staff and other friends to support friendships. For example, one of our friends uses this now as the first part of his orientation for any new staff – they find out who his friends are, but they also get a strong message: *this is the most important thing to me.*

Things to talk about:

Think of your support for things like relationship journals as facilitation of information that folks "own." Too often, relationship information is dependent on staff or support systems. If anything changes,

68

"Somewhere I once wrote that while illnesses are man's curse, handicaps (stigmas attached to illnesses) are his invention. I wondered then when will we learn the difference between what we must endure and what we bring upon ourselves. I complained that while we still have lots to learn about illnesses, we seem to have everything to learn about handicaps; that while not all illnesses have effective treatments; all handicaps are preventable and curable. Handicaps are a condition of the soul."

such as staff leaving, or folks with disabilities changing service providers, or some-thing happens to the family contact, vital information can get lost.

If the information belongs to the person, it stays with that person no matter what changes occur.

Almost everyone we met through the Personal Supports Project had a list of people they had lost contact with. But don't lose hope, because we have had almost 100% success in contacting those 'lost' people and reuniting them.   The only person who actually said no to a re-connection, came back a year later to explain why.

We have also incidentally found, while facilitating these reunions with the folks we support, that we have had a great deal of success in reuniting with people in our own lives.

Questions to discuss:

Who would you like to add to your relationship journal? Does your journal work for you?

Are there people folks would want to re-establish contact with? What are some ideas to find and contact these people? (for us, parents were a great resource – they'd kept track of their children's old friends but assumed because agencies hadn't asked we didn't care.)

Things to practice:

Personalize your relationship journal until it is perfect for you.

Go over your journal regularly and keep it updated.

Things to try:

Go through your address book, adding entries to your journal as you go along. As you are going through your address book, take note of anyone you haven't spoken to for a while and make a point to contact them.

Pick one person whose contact information you have found and phone or email them. Once you have re-connected, don't forget to add them to your relationship journal.

My Relationship Journal

	This person's name is:
(insert photo)	Phone number:
	Address:
	Email:
	Birthday:

The relationship I share with this person is:

_____
_____
_____

Our favourite activities together are:

_____
_____
_____

This is how our relationship began:

_____
_____
_____

What I like most about this person is:

_____
_____
_____

This is how others can support me with this relationship (eg. who initiates contact? Does someone provide support with visits / outings?)

_____
_____
_____

Dream a friend! (20)

We love the PATH process, a graphic planning process invented by Jack Pierpoint, Marsha Forest, Judith Snow and John O'Brien. When we do the graphic facilitation for a PATH we like to talk about leaving some blank space for "what might happen – something you don't expect, that you can't predict – a surprise from the universe – a dream come true."

We adopted this idea from a grandmother who was at a PATH meeting that was going really well in terms of helping the person plan for some important changes in their life. The grandmother stood up and said, "What about some white space? You're filling up the world of possibilities and leaving no room for surprises! I hate to think what my life would be like if I'd only got what I planned for!" We're reminded a bit of one of our friends who recently said, we take the dreams of people with disabilities and turn them into goals, leaving them with no dreams (he says that David Hingsberger said this first).

Dream A Friend

What kind of friend would you like to have? What do you imagine you would do together? What's your *dream?*

Things to talk about:

When you dream a friend, it helps to consider your own life goals

72

and your needs, and then imagine the ideal person to help you attain them. Dreaming a perfect friend is about envisioning a soul mate. For some folks this might mean a steady boyfriend or girlfriend, for others, a once-a-week movie night with a buddy who really LOVES scary movies. There are no limits to the different kinds of friends people are looking for, so it is important not to let anyone impose their dreams on you. Be true to yourself and dream your own dreams!

Questions to discuss:

What kind of personality would mesh perfectly with yours? Would you choose someone outgoing, or more laid back? What activities would you do together? How often would you want to see your friend? Is there already someone in your life that seems like they might be a great match?

Things to practise:

Brainstorm a list of perfect traits for your dream friend. Add new traits to your list as they come up.

> "For a long time, we thought those with more severe disability could not learn; now we know we did not yet know how to teach. Similarly, what we call the inability of persons to communicate may very well be our ineptness in listening."
>
> **Gunnar Dybwad**

Remember your list, just like our dreams, should always be a work in progress.

Have a conversation with your support network about where you might meet someone with those traits, and write your ideas down.

73

For example, if you are looking for someone who loves jazz, you could put 'volunteer with the Jazz Society', or 'take part in the yearly Jazz Festival', on your list.

Things to try:

After you have done this exercise as a group, start to really pay attention to the people you see while you are out and about.

Start going regularly to one of the places you think your dream friend could be. Is there anyone there that you think might be the person you are looking for?

TIP:

Go to www.inclusion.com, or Google 'PATH facilitation' to find out more about this fun and powerful planning tool created by the folks at Inclusion Press.   Every year Jack and his friends put together a "Summer Institute" where they teach the process in Toronto – put it on your dream list!   So far we've never met anyone who regretted the week they spent there.

Support your local amateur sports teams (21)

Susan comes from a sports loving family so she's the expert on this idea.   Find out the schedule for the soccer or softball league in your area and pick a team to support – or take in a hockey game at the local arena. Universities and high schools have a variety of sporting events all year long. Check out minor league sports. Become a fan!

Keep showing up and you'll get to know the other spectators. Get the shirt, wave the flag, make signs.

Things to talk about:

Kids in sports love to have people come out and cheer for them. And their parents are always glad to have someone new to talk to!

The same fans are at all the games, so there is plenty of opportunity to connect. This is a great way to get to know people.

Questions to discuss:

What are the sporting events in your neighbourhood? Are you an all-weather fan, or do you prefer indoor sports? Are there people in your group who are already active sports fans? Could you connect with anyone to go and cheer with?

Things to practise:

Rehearse what you might say to break the ice with one of the other fans. Sports fans love to talk about sports, so you might want to practice one or two sports-related anecdotes before the first game.

Go on-line or look in your neighbourhood newspaper to see what games are coming up. You could pick a team to back now, or wait until you've watched a few games.

Things to try:

Go to a game. Say hi to one person there.

> **"If you don't like the way the world is, you change it. You have an obligation to change it You just do it one step at a time."**
>
> **Marian Wright Edelman**

If you were too shy to say hi to someone, how would you feel about starting off just with eye contact and a smile?

TIP:

Sporting Goods stores are great places to ask about local teams and upcoming games.

Notice other people who are alone (22)

We might think we're the loneliest person in the room, but we're usually wrong. In fact, many people are lonely. And many are too shy to take the first step in getting to know someone new.

If you see someone sitting alone, take responsibility for introducing yourself and asking if you can join them – later on they might tell you how much it meant to them.

Things to talk about:

Think of it like this: all you really need to do is to change one thing. Sit with someone who's alone – they may become a friend.

Crosshatch Angel

If you sit with someone who is alone, this single change has the potential to radically improve your personal support network. Some of these folks will be so happy that you rescued them they will always have a special place in their hearts for you.

Our friend Aric became one of the most networked people we know, just from doing this one thing: he sits with someone who is alone every time he has the opportunity, even if there are people he already knows calling him over. "We'll talk later," he says. Aric knows how it feels to sit alone, and he didn't want to see anyone else in that situation. He just decided to handle it differently.

Questions to discuss:

How does it feel to go into a place, especially a crowded, social place, and sit alone?

Things to try:

The next time you're out somewhere and notice someone sitting alone, go sit with them.

Have a yard sale but make the point of it getting to know others (23)

Here we like to talk about John Lord's idea of the lens of relationship. It is less important to do things that are new than to do the things you already do differently. Imagine any of the things you already do through the lens of relationship. In other words, look at everything you do in terms of building relationships. With that in mind, what would you do differently?

> "If you were all alone in the universe with no one to talk to, no one with which to share the beauty of the stars, to laugh with, to touch, what would be your purpose in life? It is other life, it is love, which gives your life meaning. This is harmony. We must discover the joy of each other, the joy of challenge, the joy of growth."
>
> **Mitsugi Saotome**

Things to talk about:

One of our managers had her staff team practice introducing themselves to new people. After all, it's not only folks with disabilities that are shy and lonely.

At their following meeting they started talking about what they would do differently to work toward their goal of assisting the folks they

77

support to build their personal networks. That Jon needed to get rid of some of the stuff he'd collected was a great opportunity (but you could pick, literally, anything) - they decided to have a yard sale where the goal was to get to know the neighbours. The practiced, the staff and Jon and his friends, introducing themselves. They made nametags. They made posters that said "Jon is having a yard sale!" They made the yard inviting by putting out chairs and, on the day of the sale, Jon met people at the gate, introduced himself and gave them lemonade and a cookie. They left out some name tags for neighbours and some people wrote out their name and wore them. People felt welcomed to come into the yard, and to sit and chat.

After the yard sale, they left the chairs out, and some the neighbours are now regular visitors.

Questions to discuss:

Do you have some stuff you would like to sell? Is your garage or basement cluttered?

How could you set up your place to be really inviting to your neighbours? How could you make your neighbours feel comfortable enough to come back for further visits?

Things to practise:

Generate a list of what you would do if you wanted to have a yard sale (or a different event) where the point was getting to know your neighbours.

> **"If you want to go fast,"** says an African proverb, **"go alone. If you want to go far, go together."**
>
> **From John T. Cacioppo and William Patrick**
> *http://scienceofloneliness.com*

Things to try:

One of local govern-ment offices liked this idea so much they hosted a parking lot sale and had lots of tables, amateur clowns, popcorn, games for kids.   The folks they served got to meet others, and the neighbours of the office got to meet some of the folks served. Some of the ideas Jon and his team had were: putting up signs, placing ads in their neighbourhood newspapers, serving refreshments, wearing name tags, and providing name tags for their visitors.

If you want, you could invite other neighbours to participate in the sale.

TIPS: To learn more about the lens of relationship, pick up *Pathways to Inclusion: Building a New Story with People and Communities*, by John Lord and Peggy Hutchinson.

Have a meeting with your supporters about your friends, and make a plan (24)

How much we respect our friend and mentor John Lord is probably evident when we quote him in two sections! John says, in his book *Pathways to Inclusion*, "The time for new options that focus on social inclusion is now." It is time for us to think of some new relationship-building options and some of these might be more conscious than we assumed we'd need. Although building relationships is something that we don't usually plan for, it definitely does work out better if you have a plan.

Questions to discuss:

How would you set up a meeting to talk about friends? Who could you invite? What do you want to talk about?

Things to practise:

Brainstorm a list of people to invite. Include friends, family and

79

other supporters.

Make another list of important topics to cover in your meeting. These might include: goals for how to grow your personal support network; who to involve; favourite activities; first steps toward friendship; who you might like to connect or reconnect with.

Shadow

Things to try:

Have an initial meeting with a smaller group of trusted allies. Learn what you can from your smaller meeting to fine tune the agenda for your bigger meeting.

Now have the friendship conversation with your whole network.

Involve your family in the planning (25)

At one of our workshops, everyone accidently brought their Grandmas. It was an "accident" because what happened was the organizers forgot to invite participants – so there was this amazing space, us, and we were prepared. So when they called around to say that anyone could come, the people available were mostly grandparents. It was one of the best workshops we've ever been involved in. The best and most refreshing ideas came from the Grandmas – partly because, as seniors, they have already had to deal with their own mobility issues, or those of their friends, and also they've often rethought their own lives. As well, retirees often have more time to do some of the actual support, which is helpful.

This has led to one of our own strategies to think through problems – "What would a grandma do?"

Interestingly, they also had a different attitude about risk, perhaps because they have had their own kids grow up - getting into trouble the way kids do – and end up just fine. Grandparents seem to better understand the dignity in risk-taking; in allowing folks to make their own decisions and take responsibility for the outcome.

Things to talk about:

Often, families have long memories of who you knew and what you said in the past. They have some of the best ideas – and they're looking for ways to be helpful. Besides parents and siblings, some of the strongest leaders are grandparents and children.

Sometimes when we talk about building personal support networks, folks have the idea that we are just talking about making friends. But families should be seen as an integral part of anyone's network. Often, families are out there waiting in the wings, hoping to be invited to join in, but not wanting to interfere.

Crowd

Many families have been made to feel that they get in the way of paid "professionals." It is important families clearly know they are wanted and needed. In another meeting we asked that the fellow's nephews be invited – he had told us how important they were, and

81

they'd never been to a planning meeting for him. They had the best ideas, and they also had a lot of resources that surprised their parents. The fellow was also far more likely to try some new things (which were hard for him) with his nephews.

Have the conversations necessary to pave the way for full inclusion of families in your network!

Questions to discuss:

How can we make families feel welcome?

How do we teach our staff that it is okay to step back enough to allow family relationships to blossom? This is a tough but important conversation to have with groups of paid supporters who are natural caretakers, and who do not want to appear to be lazy.

Things to practise:

Plan a meeting of your support network and your family, with the goal being to improve communication and pave the way to a better understanding of your social needs.

Things to try:

> **"If you want things to be different, perhaps the answer is to become different yourself."**
>
> **Norman Vincent Peale**

Bring family and staff together to talk about any barriers to their full inclusion. Be open and honest about the issues, always remembering to keep things positive and hopeful.

In our experience, everyone wants the best for the folks at the centre of their network. And although it can be difficult, working together through any misunderstandings is an important step in that direction, and one that families appreciate.

Get to know your neighbours (26)

Friendships can start with a smile and a wave. If you have lived in the same neighbourhood for a while you probably have neighbours that you see regularly. A friendly wave can lead to a hello. A hello might lead to a lifelong friendship.

Things to talk about:

There are many ways to get to know our neighbours better, like our earlier suggestion about having a garage sale where the focus is getting to know your neighbours.

Getting started can be as simple as going jogging at the same time each morning, or taking a daily walk at the same time in the afternoon.

People who know their neighbours feel safer and have a greater sense of community, two things that are known to improve every aspect of quality of life, from health to finances. Check out www.scienceofloneliness.com to get an idea of the wonderful research collected in the book, *Loneliness: Human Nature and the Need for Social Connection* by John T. Cacioppo and William Patrick. After reading this book you won't wonder what's most important in life any more!

Often there is less sense of community in the larger urban centres. It might take a little more effort and time to break the ice in a bigger city, but remember it is worth it! In Chicago a group of neighbours and city planners created the amazing Neighbours Project which is always inspiring and educational www.neighborsproject.org

Questions to discuss:

Are there neighbours that you already have a budding relationship

83

with? What could you do to advance from the level of acquaintance to friendship?

Are there neighbourhood activities you enjoy that you could make more regular – again, same place, same time? Do you say hello? Do you do your part to keep your community clean and safe? Do you like pets? Could you offer to walk a dog for someone, or offer your assistance feeding their goldfish when they go away on vacation? Could you offer to water their plants for them?

Is there a neighbourhood association you could join?

Things to practise:

Make a list of five things you could do to get to know your neighbours better. Pick one thing from your list that you can do in the next week.

Things to try:

Notice whether there are any seniors in your area who might need help in the garden, or carrying groceries. Be creative in your neighbourliness.

Have an open house and invite the neighbours in (27)

The main ideas of the open house are to be hospitable, and to have a welcoming home where neighbours will be comfortable to come and visit.

Sun

Have some snacks and drinks

84

available. Make your place inviting by leaving out some things you could use to start a conversation.

Things to talk about:

Think about how you will let your neighbours know about your open house. You could invite them person-ally, or deliver nice in-vitations door-to-door.

On the day of the open house you could put up signs and balloons.

You will want to make sure your gate is open, and that your place is easy to find and looks inviting. You might want to get some balloons and/or some flowers to give your place a party atmosphere.

Don't forget to have some fun things around - like toys, games, or puzzles - for kids to play with. Our friend Mishel is so good at this and always has these amazing, simple entertaining ideas on how to keep people interacting.   She lines up kids to squirt whipped cream in their mouths and brings out a blow torch to finish the meringue on the lemon pie – it's a bit messy but memorable!

Questions to discuss:

Is your home as inviting as it could be? What could you do to make it more hospitable? What will you need to prepare for before the open house? Is there any baking, cleaning, or shopping to do?

Things to practise:

Rehearse introducing yourself. How you will greet your neighbours when they arrive?

Things to try:

Pick a Saturday or Sunday afternoon (a time when most of your neighbours won't be working). Give yourself enough time between

85

giving out your invitations and having your open house to comfortably get prepared, but not so much time that your neighbours forget all about it.

TIPS: If you are in turn invited to a neighbour's open house, or house warming party, bring a small gift, like a plant, a bouquet of flowers, or some fresh home baking.

Read your community newspapers (28)

The smaller local papers tend to focus on neighbourhoods. They are a great way to find out what is happening in your community.

Things to talk about:

Community newspapers are often full of 2 for 1 coupons for restaurants and events, making activities more affordable and promoting the idea of inviting someone to join you.

> "What man actually needs is not a tensionless state but rather the striving and struggling for some goal worthy of him. What he needs is not the discharge of tension at any cost, but the call of a potential meaning waiting to be fulfilled by him."
>
> **Victor Frankl**

You can find listings of local activities, movies, music, theatre, and volunteer opportunities.

Questions to discuss:

What kinds of things do you like to do? Who would you invite for a 2 for 1 meal or movie?

Things to try:

Bring in a copy of your community newspaper for everyone in the group and look through it together. See what you can find.

If each person picks one event and chooses who they are going to invite to join them, then they will be prepared to make their invitation.

Call your friend!

Deliver the community newspaper (29)

Now that you have had a closer look through your local paper, perhaps you'd think about taking on a paper route. What better way to meet neighbours than to walk regularly throughout your neighbourhood. Besides that, having a job is a great way to bring in some more money, make some co-worker friends and feel better about yourself.

Things to talk about:

Take on a smaller route so that you have time to stop and chat with people.

This is a good time to talk about how work makes us feel. People are proud of their jobs; indeed our jobs are often become a major contributor to who we are as people. Many of us make long-lasting friendships with people from work.

Questions to discuss:

How would you apply for a local paper delivery route?

How big a route would you feel comfortable taking on, keeping in mind that one of the main goals of the job is to be able to stop and chat with your neighbours?

Things to practise:

Get to know your current paper delivery person and ask them how

87

to apply.

Walk around your neighbourhood to get a feel for the size of route you might want. Imagine yourself stopping and talking to the occasional customer.

The Corrections

What might you say to the folks you see on your route?

Things to try:

Apply for a paper route. Once you're assigned a route, do a few practice runs. Take note of the place at each house where you think the occupant might want their paper delivered. Your customers will appreciate that you take care that their paper doesn't get wet, or end up in the bushes. Don't be the delivery person who just throws the paper in the general direction of the house and then runs on to the next house.

Start delivering!

Join a church or synagogue, or find some other spiritual gathering place (30)

Brian was considered one of the most connected people in a small community, even though he'd moved there as an adult and had no speech. Brian's mom told us that how she made these connections was to join a church and volunteer Brian and herself to hand out the church newsletter (she said, really, she just put up her hand the first time they asked for a volunteer). Before long, there was a line-up of people waiting to chat with Brian every Sunday, "and no one wants to be in my line-up!" she said.   "And that's just great!"

Another person we know went to the same church for two years and felt quite ignored. With some support she decided to talk to the minister. She told him that she didn't feel like she was a welcome part of the congregation. It became clear that the minister perceived her as an "eternal child" and assumed she would only take part in the children's activities.

As an adult she was upset to hear this, but she was also proud of herself for overcoming her fears and talking to the minister. And she was happy in the end, because she started going to a new church where the pastor and the congregation welcomed her as a full member, including her in every aspect of their ministry.

Things to talk about:

This can be an important way for folks to make connections.

Remember that if you give one church a try and it is not working for you, you have options.

Questions to discuss:

What churches, synagogues, or other spiritual meeting places are in your area?

Universe of Stories

Things to practise:

Go for a walk around your neighbourhood and make a list of the churches. Take note of the ones that seem more welcoming to you. See if there is a newsletter you could take home to read.

Don't discount churches where the congregation is of another culture. If you know someone in your community who goes to church, ask them about it. Maybe you could go with them.

Things to try:

Pick a church and start going. Give it a fair chance, but keep the conversation alive about whether it is the right place for you.

TIP: Local newspapers often have a "Sunday section" listing churches and service times. As the facilitator, make sure you mention all kinds of religions and get some sense of who is in the room. We've found that people with disabilities who are Jewish, for example, don't often get chances to talk about this aspect of their life and are really excited to share their heritage.

Take advantage of the social opportunities at your place of worship (31)

Now that you have picked a church or other place of worship that you think is a good fit for you – don't stop there. Arriving just in time for the service and leaving right after might fulfill your spiritual needs, but it doesn't take care of your social needs.

> **"The most important thing to remember is this: To be ready at any moment to give up what you are for what you might become."**
>
> **W.E.B. DuBois**

Things to talk about:

Find out how you can be a more involved member of the congregation or group. Many churches have social functions like bake sales and thrift sales. One church we know of has a kids' drama club, where children can get involved in theatre, and adult volunteers help out with the production.

So, stay for coffee hour and introduce yourself to the person in charge. Stick around after the service and chat with people. Find out what social activities are available for you. Offer to wash dishes!

Think about how this idea might be used in other social groups you belong to.

Questions to discuss:

What kinds of social activities interest you? Does your church have a newsletter with information about upcoming events?
Things to practise:

Role play talking to the pastor or the rabbi at your chosen place of worship. How will you introduce yourself? Prepare yourself to have a conversation about how you might take part in social events.

Things to try:

If you are too shy to approach the person in charge by yourself, try asking someone in your network to help you.

Remember, places of worship are all about bringing people together. Most spiritual leaders are more than happy to have folks take part in their social activities. You have valuable skills to offer and volunteers are normally welcomed with open arms.

If not, is it time to try a different church or synagogue?

Be true to yourself (32)

Be proud of who you are and show people you can stand up for

91

what you believe in. People need to like you for who you are.

The more true friendships you have, the stronger your self-esteem. And the stronger your self-esteem, the easier it is to stick up for yourself.

Don't compromise yourself or your beliefs just to be accepted.

Keep in mind, being a friend is the opposite of being a bully.

Things to talk about:

We've found a lot of information on not being a bully, or dealing with bullies, but very little about how to be good friend. Good friend thinking and skills-building does away with bullying because there's no longer any room for it. Part of what makes a good and lasting friendship is a mutual acceptance of who we are and what we believe in.

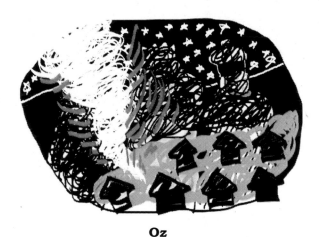

Oz

Bullies are aggressive and intimidating; friends are accepting and supportive.

Questions to discuss:

What does it mean to be a good friend? Why is it important to be true to ourselves? Is it worth having a friend who insists that you give up on your values or beliefs; one who makes you feel bad about yourself?

How do bullies make us feel? Why do you think some people are bullies?

This is a good time to talk about safety. When is it better to just walk away from a situation?

Things to practise:

Have groups role play being proud and standing up for themselves in situations where someone is trying to bully them.

Have individuals take turns being the true friend and being the bully. The bully should try to get the friend to do something they are not comfortable with.

Afterwards, discuss how does each of these roles make people feel.

What are you good at? Teach a skill that you love (33)

A friend of ours loves computers. As a way of meeting people and sharing his skills, he arranged a small dedicated space in the offices of a local organization and started up a computer lab. They put out a self-serve sign-up sheet and took appointments and he would teach folks how to start up a computer, how to use email, and a number of other computer basics. He thought he didn't know that much, but as it turned out, he knew more than most and as he continued, he found himself learning more and more so that he could answer all their questions. People were really thankful for his help.

Things to talk about:

Discussing and teaching our skills is a great way to boost our self-esteem. It reminds us to focus on our strengths and our gifts. It can be really powerful. Our friend Nancy, after years of professional augmentative communication supports, started teaching others how to use the Ipad to communicate – she was excited to go from experiencer of services to mentor. Other friends

93

started up an Ipad for Communication group that meets regularly.

Have folks come up with at least one thing that they might feel comfortable teaching others. It could be figuring out bus routes, using a digital camera or those impossible TV remote controls, baking, household chores, growing a vegetable garden – it could be anything. Be creative.

Sharing our gifts through teaching makes us feel like we are needed.

Questions to discuss:

Brainstorm what the people in your group good at? How could they share their knowledge in a way that allows them to build relationships? Often people won't know that a thing they're skilled at might be something that others would like them to teach.

Things to try:

Let people know that you have a skill that you would be willing to teach. If necessary, ask someone from your support network help you to get started. Now, be a teacher!

Be patient and friendly, and you will soon see that your students are glad to have you in their lives.

TIP: Remember your affirmations! If you need a reminder about affirmations, go back to number 6.

Go to the gym (34)

Going to the gym is a great way to meet people. Once again, doing the same thing, at the same place, at the same time every week, you will no doubt get to know the other regulars.

Things to talk about:

Exercising regularly is something a lot of people do. If you are just starting out, many gyms offer personal training to ensure you are working out safely. This is a great way to get to know the staff at your gym. By the time you have a set exercise routine, you will have noticed some of the other regulars. Check out the activity schedule on the next page. This schedule is great to use at the gym, because it not only asks what you did and who was there, but also what the relationship opportunities were.

> **"For no matter what we achieve, if we don't spend the vast majority of our time with people we love and respect, we cannot possibly have a great life. But if we spend the vast majority of our time with people we love and respect – people we really enjoy being on the bus with and who will never disappoint us – then we will almost certainly have a great life, no matter where the bus goes. The people we interviewed from the good-to-great companies clearly loved what they did, largely because they loved who they did it with."**
>
> **Jim Collins**

Questions to discuss:

Besides being a great way to meet new people, exercising improves our health and makes us feel better about ourselves. If you are just deciding to get into shape, discuss your plans with your doctor first.

Which gym is best for

95

you? Is there one in your neighbourhood that you'd like to try?

Community centre gyms often have lower rates for folks on a fixed income.

Things to practise:

Try dropping in to your gym of choice before joining. Most gyms will allow you to "try before you buy."

Things to try:

Join a gym and attend regularly. Start off easy, and slowly build up your workout routine. The worst thing you can do is over-train on your first few days. Nothing turns folks off of exercise more than intensely sore muscles from overdoing it at the beginning.

Say hi to the other regulars. Perhaps there is someone there that you think you might like to work out with, or go for coffee with afterwards.

Week at a glance for (name) _____   Date: _____

	Monday	Tuesday	Wednesday	Thursday	Friday	Saturday	Sunday
Morning activity							
Location							
Accompanied by							
Contacts							
Afternoon activity							
Location							
Accompanied by							
Contacts							
Evening activity							
Location							
Accompanied by							
Contacts							

Learn to say "hello" in different languages (35)

This is a fun one to do with a group of self-advocates. It is a powerful thing for facilitators to realize that folks with disabilities often know much more than we think they know. This is certainly true of languages. In our experience, people know a lot of languages.

Facilitators can prepare ahead of time by learning hello in a few different languages. Learn how to sign hello and goodbye.

Things to talk about:

We are always amazed how many languages people know, including sign language. Ask how many people in your group know 'hello' in any languages other than English. As a facilitator, you might wonder about how many opportunities people with disabilities who are in services have to speak their language or talk about their culture – connections lots of us from other cultures take for granted.

Questions to discuss:

Do you already know the word for hello in any other languages?

Do you have any neighbours who speak other languages?

Things to practise:

Ask the people in your group how they would say hello to a deaf person. If no one knows, teach them.

Have the folks who know the word hello in other languages teach the rest.

Have people make a list so that they can continue to practice the words they've learned.

When you use the words regularly, you will soon have them memorized!

Things to try:

Greet a neighbour in their own language. Greet your local shop-keepers. Teach what you know to others.

Try a new look – see who says hello (36)

In our workshops we sometimes show a picture of a group of guys with Mohawk haircuts wearing black leather jackets with skulls on them.

One day Aaron's neighbour, Ethel, was with him and they watched his son walking up the street, coming home with a new Mohawk and a jacket made out of rubber and duct tape. Ethel said "You know, I think back to when I raised my children and all the conversations I had with them about what I didn't like about their hair. I wish now," she went on, "that I had said what I really meant to say, which was, 'I love you.'"

Things to talk about:

A new look can bring new friendship opportunities. It can be a new haircut, a hat, a new outfit, or a whole new look.

In being accepting of differences, we need to remember not to prejudge people who dress differently than we do. It is the person that counts.

Questions to discuss:

Do you have a look in mind for yourself that you have always wanted to try out?

Do you know anyone who has the kind of look you'd like for yourself? Could they help you? Our friend Amanda loves to do makeovers for her friends and they appreciate how hard she studies all the techniques and keeps up on makeup brands.

This is a good time to discuss what kinds of looks don't attract friends. For example, does poor hygiene attract people to us?

Things to practise:

When you are out in the community, take note of all the different looks people have.

Look through magazines for new hairstyles or fashion tips.

Go out and try on different clothes, or hats, or sunglasses. Be open to trying some that you think you won't like – after all, you never know for sure until you try....

If you are due for new prescription glasses, take a friend with you to the optometrist and try on some new frames.

Decide on a new look for yourself.

Things to try:

Now that you have decided on a new look, this part is easy. Go to the salons and/or the clothing stores and take the plunge!

Notice whether different people are talking to you now. Who is complimenting you on your new style?

TIPS:

Hair stylists usually have great ideas about what you might do and they have photo magazines of modern hairstyles.

Have one good joke you can tell (37)

Laughter really is the best medicine.

Humour is now being incorporated into many different therapies. In fact, our good friend, Shelley Nessman, teaches laughter yoga. Laughter can lower stress levels, improve tolerance to pain, and has balancing effects on many of our bodies' functions. If you don't believe us, give it a try!

In the short term, a good joke can break the ice and make people around us feel more comfortable.

Things to talk about:

Often in our workshops we talk about "family jokes" – the kinds of jokes that family or good friends have which they understand, but people outside their circle might not know. These are the kinds of jokes that affirm our relationships. Self-advocate Barb Goode, in her book, *The Goode Life: Memoirs of Disability Rights Activist Barb Goode* has some great examples of fun family jokes she shared with her dad.

Many studies show that we are more prone to laughter when we are with people in our close social networks. The more comfortable we are with folks, the easier it is for us to let go. This has a building positive effect as our comfort levels improve, and as our networks grow.

Questions to discuss:

Why is it fun to share jokes?

Who do you know who is a good joke-teller?

101

Things to practise:

Pick one joke and practice it so that you're ready when there's an uncomfortable gap in the conversation – be known as the person who makes everyone feel comfortable!

Bring along a joke book if telling jokes isn't your gift. Aaron admits that he can only ever remember one joke at a time. But that's okay - one joke is all it takes to help make folks feel more at ease.

Here are a couple of jokes to get you started.

Doctor, Doctor I keep thinking I'm a dog.
Sit on the couch and we will talk about it.
But I'm not allowed up on the couch!

Here is Aaron's one joke:

Knock. Knock. Who's there? Banana.
Knock. Knock. Who's there? Banana.
Knock. Knock. Who's there? Orange- orange you glad I didn't say banana?

Do you have some good jokes to share?

Things to try:

Tell your joke at the first opportunity. Remember, jokes are often contagious. If you tell one, chances are that others will share their jokes too.

Try injecting more humour into your next week and see how that goes. Also, if someone is making you laugh, tell them how much you enjoy their sense of humour.

TIPS: Check out www.laughteryoga.org for more information.

Google "joke of the day" and choose from about 37 million different daily joke websites.

Take photos and show them around (38)

Make albums, frame your pictures, upload them to online sites, use your computer's slide show function – share your experiences and your visions.

Things to talk about:

We believe that photos are one of the best tools ever for the development of relationships. Photos around the house of our friends and the people who care about us are great conversation starters and are also constant affirmations of our best selves.

In our original personal networks project we accidentally discovered the power of photos. We wanted to write a report that had lots of pictures in it, because we thought that would be more fun for people to read. So we handed out disposable cameras.

The folks we were supporting took those cameras out into their communities to places they'd gone to for years, to people they'd interacted with for years, and asked to take their pictures. People would say "Why would you want my picture?" and it became a great opportunity to talk about how important they were in the person's life, which led to deepening those connections.

People were very moved by being asked for photos – 100% of the people we asked were happy to have their photos taken, and delighted to know how important they are to the folks taking the pictures.

This can be something that people can be uncomfortable with at first. You might want to take smaller steps. For example, you could bring along a trusted person from your network for moral support,

103

or you could decide to ask just one person to begin with.

Have a vision of what you want and slowly lean in that direction.

Questions to discuss:

What are some of your favourite photos?

Do you know anyone who is a good photographer? Perhaps they could give you a few pointers.

Things to practise:

Get people to prepare for this section by bringing in photos of themselves and their friends and talking about them. What are the feelings that are in the photos?

Folks could bring in their own cameras as well. They could take pictures of other people in the group, or whatever they want!

Things to try:

Go take some more photos! Make a collage! Join a photography club! Enter photo competitions!

If you are a member of a social website like TYZE or Facebook you could upload a photo, or an album of photos, to share with your friends.

TIPS: Digital cameras allow you to try all kinds of different photography. You simply delete the ones that don't turn out. This kind of picture-taking practice is a great learning tool for making your photographs interesting and memorable.

One of the folks who came to a workshop showed us how she uses her digital camera as a kind of diary, to document an event or a meeting with a friend, which she then takes on to the next event or friend and begins that interaction by showing them what's on her camera's memory.   A great assistive communication technique!

Be aware of the different privacy settings for your social website. Do you want to share your photos just with your friends, or with everyone? Choose your privacy settings accordingly

Stay on top of some current events and look for opportunities to discuss them (39)

Whether it is politics that interest you, or entertainment news, or whatever, you can connect with people by discussing what you've read in the paper or on-line, or seen on television.

Things to talk about:

Most people are interested in talking about current events.

Many people have specific interests. One of the people in our networks is a Brittney Spears expert. She knows everything about Brittney! And she has found that almost everyone is interested in finding out what is new for the pop superstar!

Does anyone in your group know someone who is an expert in any current events?

Questions to discuss:

Do you watch entertainment news? Do you read about current events in the papers or on-line? What specific interests do you have that you could learn more about and share?

Do you, or does anyone in your network, know people with similar interests?

How will you find opportunities to talk about your interests?

Things to practise:

105

Watch the news on television, or read it in the newspapers or on the internet. Keep tabs on the weather forecasts.

Pick something from the news that really interests you and become an expert!

Rehearse chatting about news that interests you.

Things to try:

Next time you're out, mention something newsworthy that you have learned. Or break the ice by chatting with someone about your favourite movie star or TV reality show.

TIPS: The internet is a great place to find different takes on the same news items. If you get your news on-line from a variety of sources and from a variety of perspectives, you can expand your knowledge with a just few clicks of your mouse.

Go to the local pub to watch the game instead of watching it at home alone (40)

By now you will have noticed that one of the main themes of *101 Ways . . .* is to put yourself out there. Rather than sitting at home alone watching sports, find a sports pub and mingle with other sports fans.

Things to talk about:

Sharing your love of sports is a great way to connect with people that have the same interests as you. Wearing the right jersey might start a conversation, and a conversation is a step in the direction of friendship!

Questions to discuss:

106

What sports do you like? Which teams do you follow?

Is there a sports pub in your neighbourhood?

What are some good sports related conversation starters?

Things to practise:

Have the sports fans in your group pair off and practice having conversations about their favourite sports/teams.

Things to try:

Pick a pub, and then go out to watch your favourite sports with other fans. If you have a team jersey, wear it. See if anyone mentions it. Our friend Jenna has collected dozens of photos of herself wearing team jerseys and meeting hockey stars, who have signed her jersey. She's recently started a blog about her life and her interest in hockey.

Try sharing your sports knowledge with someone who is cheering for the same team.

At home afterwards, talk about what went well and what you might do differently next time.

TIPS: Read the sports page of your local newspaper.

Many sports pubs have sports trivia games that you can play with other fans. Have fun while building on your expertise!

Family members can be friends too (41)

When thinking about your personal support network, don't forget to include your family. Also, think about the people in your extended family – siblings, cousins, aunts, uncles, nieces, nephews, grandparents....

Think about the family relationships you might like to deepen.

Things to talk about:

Families are often very receptive to being involved, but can be feel like they are getting in the way. It is important for our entire support network to make our families feel needed and wanted.

In British Columbia many people have microboards, a group of family and friends who get together to support a person with a disability. They form a small non-profit society to focus on assisting the person at the centre in their planning and support needs. We've noticed, when talking to people about starting a board, that they are so excited to be involved and have an effective role – and glad to know who else would be involved.

Questions to discuss:

Are there members of your family who might feel excluded from your support network?

Is there anyone in your family with whom you have lost contact? Would you like to re-connect with them? How will you do that?

How can you make your family members feel welcomed into your inner circle?

One of our friends who supports people with disabilities used the need for a new washing machine to involve family member. She could have just gone to the department store and made her best guess about which one to buy, but instead asked the family member for help in purchasing the new appliance. This happened to be a type of connection that the family member felt very comfortable with, and by the time the washing machine arrived, a door had opened for future participation. It made the person's family member feel needed and wanted, and it helped to deepen their relationship.

Things to practise:

Look up their contact information. You can try the phone book, other relatives, or the internet. Are there any other ways that you could find out their contact information. We've been so surprised by the second and third cousins who've shown up looking for their lost relative, and even grandparents.

These types of conversations can be very emotional, but they are well worth having. If you are having a hard time getting started, ask a trusted person for their help.

Things to try:

Call up a family member you would like to reconnect with. Invite them for a coffee and tell them that you would like to have them take part in your support network. You will find that most people are happy to help and have just been waiting to be asked.

Take a multi-cultural cooking class (42)

Lots of schools have adult education classes, many of which include different cooking classes. Taking a multi-cultural cooking class exposes folks to different cultures and different delicious foods. Go into your local community centre and pick up their course guide or a school board continuing education booklet. These course listings are often available on-line as well. You can check in your local newspaper too. Look for the culinary arts sections.

Cooking courses are inexpensive and fun.

Things to talk about:

This is a perfect opportunity to talk about hospitality – about how food changes everything. Sharing meals is a great way to bring people closer. It is an intimate act that promotes friendship and conversation.

Questions to discuss:

What kind of dishes have you always wanted to learn how to make?

Do you go out for multi-cultural meals?

Do you have friends from other cultures? Would you like to make friends from other cultures?

It Gets Better Heart

Things to practise:

See what cooking classes are available to you. Then pick a few multi-cultural restaurants from those cultures and go out for meals. Decide which are your favourites, and then choose a class.

Things to try:

Sign up for a class and start cooking. Pair up with someone in the class, and think about inviting them over to try out what you have learned.

At the end of the course, think about signing up for another one. Maybe your current partner will be interested in signing up with you.

Celebrate all the holidays (43)

Wear green on St. Patrick's Day and meet Irish people; give out heart-shaped cookies for Valentines; be the spirit of Christmas present... make everything you do be about potential connections.

Things to talk about:

Holidays are times of celebration. People seem more open to connections during holidays.

Questions to discuss:

What holidays do people like? What are their favourite things to do?

Things to practise:

Mark the holidays on your calendar. Give yourself enough advance notice to get ready. You might need time to get your baking done, wash all your green clothes, write your cards, get new batteries for your musical Santa Claus pin – to prepare for whatever you plan to do to celebrate.

Make a list of what you might do for each holiday.

Things to try:

Decide how you will celebrate the next holiday, even if it's one people don't usually celebrate. Get prepared and do it. See how many people mention your effort.

Put "friends and family" at the top of the agenda for planning meetings (44)

111

> **"New Story is grounded in the principles of citizenship. However, we have learned that for citizenship to be meaningful for consumers, families, providers, and policy, it must be explicitly framed around self-determination and community.**
>
> **"Self-determination – the belief that all citizens desire to have choice and control in their lives, especially over the disability supports they require. This would include having voice and choice in all things in one's life, including personal development, employment, recreation, and education.**
>
> **"Community – the belief that all human beings desire to belong and participate with others in families, neighbourhoods, networks and groups."**
>
> **"Building a New Story Transforming Disability Supports and Policies: Re-Visiting In Unison"**
>
> *A commentary by:*
> *John Lord, Judith Snow and Charlotte Dinawall*

Things to talk about:

We've talked about how John Lord sees the idea of a "lens of relationship," that we can see anything and everything we do through a different lens, that actually makes more sense, if we make the attempt.

We were talking to John once several years ago about some issue and thinking, "Well, we could help with that, for sure... we could do this, and then we could do that... we could fix everything."

John asked, "Who should be there with you to help with this?"

We said, "Oh, it will be simple – we can fix this issue on our own."

John said, "Well, then the person won't have the issue – it will be gone, but unless you are an involved part of their network, you'll also be gone when the problem is fixed. So, will that have answered the opportunity we have here to ask who should be involved with us? If a new friend can be involved, or if a family member or friend already in the person's network can deepen their relationship by dealing with this, then they have addressed the issue AND they have deepened their network."

As an example of this theory in action, Shari, one of Spectrum Society's managers, decided to talk about friend and family relationships at the beginning of each meeting, which changed the dynamic of all their subsequent meetings. Staff began thinking in terms of involving others. Because they started each meeting talking positively about relationships with friends and family, the focus shifted to including the entire support network. A discussion about an upcoming statutory holiday became more about how the individual might connect with his family, and less about who would work the holiday. And the staff having the discussion liked the clarity of what they might be doing on that holiday – some of them loved being an "honorary" family member for a dinner or a day and really wanted to be part of those shifts. Others, not so much.

It Gets Better Angel

Questions to discuss:

This an important time to let staff know that **it is okay to step back** enough to allow families and friends to get involved.

This is the time, too, to let the folks being supported

113

know that it is okay to ask their staff to step back.

How can staff, who are proud of their jobs and their support, be supported to step back without feeling like they are being perceived as lazy?

Jesse, one of Spectrum's best support workers has an uncanny ability to blend into the woodwork whenever there is an opportunity to allow friends and family to make decisions, or to build on their relationships. He's there when needed, but he never interferes when there are opportunities for new or deeper connections within the person's network. Are there people you work with who have this valuable skill? How much positive feedback do you think they get for blending in so well that, after the event, people forget they were there? This might be a good time to give them some! Of all our surprises, how very little feedback good personal network facilitators get has been one of the biggest. Evaluations often do not speak to this gift, to say the least (evaluations often speak to every gift but this!).

How can we ensure that all the folks in our support networks feel like an important part of the team?

Things to practise:

Look at everything you do through the lens of friend and family inclusion.

If there is a staff member in your support network who is expert at involving family and friends, have them talk to the rest of the team about how they do it. Bring people in from other staff teams who are good at this. Use local resources.

Things to try:

Put "Family and Friends" at the top of every meeting agenda, just for a month to try it out. Notice how the whole dynamic of these meetings shifts.

Have part of each meeting be about how staff can naturally involve friends and family in all the important decisions for the person they support. For example, if someone in the network is a whiz at electronics, how about asking them to help you set up your new stereo?

Share what you love – lend someone a book or DVD you enjoyed (45)

Things to talk about: A big part of building new friendships is looking for people who have things in common with you. Sharing books, movies, or music is a great way to communicate your passions, and passions = connections.

Gertrude and Alice

The more passionate you are about something, the greater chance that you will find other folks with the same passions.

Questions to discuss:

What movies, books or music do you love? What are your passions?

One of the Moms we know loves to trade and lend out her cookbooks. Over time, without anyone even paying much attention to it, it turned into a community cookbook trading club

115

with regular meetings and planned events.

Things to practise:

Make a list of your passions: your favourite books, DVD's, CD's. Pick one thing you won't mind lending out and prepare yourself to chat about it. Choose a partner, and practice a brief exchange about the thing you're lending. What is it about the book or movie or music you are lending that makes you so passionate about it?

Things to try:

Pick someone and lend them something you love. This act is very personal and makes people feel special.

Arrange a time to get together to talk about it.

Try lending them something else. Maybe they will lend you something they love.

TIP: If it is important to you to make sure you get your beloved book or DVD, or CD back, tell this to people when you lend them the item. It is a good idea to mark things with your name or initials. You also might keep a list of what you have lent and to whom.

The best thing, however, is to develop a 'lending relationship' with the person, in which you exchange things back and forth on a regular basis.

Finally, don't feel bad about reminding someone that they have your item; it is easy for people to forget where things came from, and it is much better to ask than it is to hold a grudge.

Make it a habit to be the one who always welcomes the new person (46)

The great thing about being welcoming is that you can do it in any

116

setting. It could be at a meeting or a social activity. It could be with new neighbours in your community. Or just be the person who welcomes new businesses into your area!

Things to talk about:

Aric, the friend we talked about back in section 22 "Notice other people who are alone" – the person who makes it a point to always sit with someone who is alone – is, of course, also a self-made expert at welcoming new people.

Most of us assume they we are the loneliest and most introverted person in a group, especially if we are new. But usually we are not.

> "Inclusion means being with one another and caring for one another. It means inviting parents, students, and community members to be part of a new culture, a new reality.
>
> . . .
>
> Inclusion means inviting those who have been left out (in anyway) to come in, and asking them to help design new systems that encourage every person to participate to the fullness of their capacity as partners and as members.
>
> *"Inclusion! The Bigger Picture"*
> **by Jack Pearpoint**
> **& Marsha Forest**

If you make it a habit to be the person who always welcomes newcomers, the people you have welcomed will often hold a special place in their heart for you. And they may, in turn, become more welcoming to others. Imagine a society where everyone is wel-coming. Look up some of the work of Marsha Forest and Jack Pierpoint and their visionary friends from Inclusion Press to get a sense of how exciting and possible this is!

Questions to discuss:

What activity do you have

coming up where you will have the opportunity to welcome someone new?

Who do you know who is very welcoming? What do you think it is that makes them that way?

What kind of body language is most welcoming? What body language makes us appear closed-off or unwelcoming?

Things to practise:

In groups of two or three, take turns welcoming each other. Be gracious and inviting. Make eye contact. When it is your turn to be the "welcomer," ask the newcomer if there is anything they need. If you are in a group of three, introduce the new person to the third person.

If you have time, try the same exercise, but don't be welcoming. How does it make the others feel when they are not welcomed?

Things to try:

The next chance you get, welcome someone new. Take note of how they respond.

Take a class at the local community centre (47)

Local community centres are great places to connect with others. They offer programs in writing, painting, music, languages, dance, fitness, photography, and much, much more. Some also offer bus tours for folks who want to go shopping or sightseeing.

Things to talk about:

We believe that inclusion is the only possibility. That segregation is a civil rights issue. That inclusion can be facilitated by choosing the right environments, focusing on gifts and building all our skills to make, in the end, a better community because of the inclusion of citizens with what Barb Goode calls, not disabilities but "diversibilities." Community centre classes are an ideal place to get involved in that they attract a wide range of people from a variety of cultures and backgrounds.

Life Of Fire

Community centre courses are low in stress and high in fun!

Questions to discuss:

What are some things that you have always wanted to learn? Are you a budding writer? Have you always been fascinated with the piano? Are you intrigued by wellness activities like tai chi, yoga, or meditation?

Things to practise:

Pick up your local community centre guide and read through it. It will list the courses offered as well as the cost and the registration details. Put a check mark beside the courses that interest you.

Things to try:

Pick one course to begin with. Choose one that interests you and that has good potential for relationships.

TIPS: Many community centres offer discounts for folks on social assistance.

Community centres are sometimes affiliated with other local centres or nearby schools that also offer programs. Their guides might also list upcoming neighbourhood activities, like runs, flea markets, and community celebrations.

Resolve conflicts peacefully and move on; don't hold a grudge (48)

We're here to make friends, not enemies. When people wish "we could all just get along," you might aspire to be the one they'll think of as a role model.

Holding a grudge generally hurts both parties. To forgive, you need to take responsibility for your part in the argument; after all it takes two to have a disagreement.

Sometimes we repeat the story of the conflict, to ourselves and to others, so often that we cannot forget. Once you decide to be forgiving, you have to let go of the negative stories. Forgive – *and forget.*

Things to talk about:

Have folks talk about times that they have resolved things and how they have done it.

Often, the grudges we hold are based on guilt, or on other things that no one has any control over. Sometimes, we cannot even remember why we were holding the grudge in the first place.

Life is too short to always be carrying around negative feelings.

Questions to discuss:

Is holding a grudge a good way to make and keep friends?

Are there people in your life you would like to forgive?

What is a first step toward forgiveness?

Things to practise:

Don't be afraid to express yourself, and be open to letting others express themselves too, but keep the focus on forgiveness.

Don't let ego and pride get in the way of your relationships.

Let's face it, every single one of us has made mistakes in our lives; Where would we be if no one had forgiven us?

Things to try:

Call someone with whom you would like to resolve a conflict. Tell them how important they are to you. Arrange a time to get together to talk things through.

Afterwards, think about how it went. Do you feel like a weight has been lifted from your shoulders?

TIP: our friend Shari shared this wonderful quote from Mark Twain, which we think fits in here perfectly: "Forgiveness is the fragrance that the violet sheds on the heel that crushed it."

Take initiative; suggest something fun or interesting (49)

Your group might have noticed by now, having had a chance to have some of the discussions and participate in some of the

121

exercices, that putting ourselves out there is not as scary as we may have originally thought. Nor is it particularly a disability issue!

It is actually more scary to think about it than it is to just do it!

So, be brave! Be fun! Be interesting!

Things to talk about:

As you get used to inviting people to do fun stuff, you'll come to see that everyone is happy to come, but hardly anyone ever makes the first move.

Every summer Aaron plans a waterside barbecue by the river or at the beach. He chooses a different place each time and cooks different food. People are delighted to come, and they often remark that he is the only one who ever plans these fun get-togethers.

If you take the initiative to suggest fun and interesting activities, you will become a role model for the people in your expanding network. People will remember you for your great ideas and they will thank you for including them in your plans.

Questions to discuss:

If you were going to try something new, something out of the ordinary, what would it be?

How about museums, the theatre, a corn maze, walking tours, an art exhibit, a farmer's market? Be creative. There is always something interesting going on!

Things to practise:

The things you choose could involve a whole group of people, or just one. It's up to you.

Things to try:

Pick something interesting and decide who to invite. Call them up ask them to join you. Give your friends as much advance notice as you can.

Think about keeping track of upcoming activities on a calendar or in your day planner. Choose a frequency that you feel comfortable with and continue to include friends in your unique and entertaining activities.

Ask the agency that supports you to make personal support networks a priority (50)

All support agencies should know that personal networks are a priority. If they don't seem to know this, people can tell them. They need to know our priorities.

Staff will be more likely to feel they have permission to focus on developing relationships if it's part of everything from job descriptions to evaluations to program monitoring.

Things to talk about:

Some staff who are good at supporting relationships, but less good at other things, report that they are regularly reprimanded for the administrative or household duties that they may not be very good at, but they are rarely praised for their support of personal relationships.

If your support agency makes relationships a priority, these staff would be valued for the network facilitation at which they excel. This should lead to a better relationship between staff and management, and may be the catalyst to staff improving in the other areas of their job performance.

123

Questions to discuss:

Do you feel supported in building and maintaining your personal support network?

Does your agency focus on relationships?

Are your staff supported to make personal networks a priority? Are you sending people who don't know how to swim out to support swimmers? Equally, are you sending people who don't know how to meet, greet and facilitate relationships out to support people to make friends and allies?

Things to practise:

Talk to your staff and other folks who are supported by your agency. Get a feel for the level of importance given to building networks.

Things to try:

At your next meeting, make the first item on the agenda "personal networks." Invite your whole team, including managers, coordinators and directors. Tell your support team that you want them to focus on helping you develop meaningful relationships. Make it clear that you want to include your family in this process.

Have these meetings on a regular basis to discuss how things are going for you. Be honest about how well things are working out.

Think about inviting a self-advocate to your meetings to discuss how they made friends and developed their networks.

Step outside of your usual circle (51)

Some of us may have gotten used to doing the same routine all the time, not to say that there isn't a place for that in our lives. After all, one of the main themes in our *101 Friends* workshops is that doing the same things at the same place and the same time every week is a great way to meet people.

Things to talk about:

What we are talking about here is shaking things up a little. Let's say, as an example, that a person's only regular and long-term activity is weekly sports training with the Special Olympics. There, they probably see the same people each week, and that is great. But, what if one week you decided to do something completely different, as well as your Special O event?

Questions to discuss:

What is your usual circle? It is good to have folks define what their usual circle is and write it down. Then ask them, what would happen if you did something outside this circle?

Are there new things you have always wanted to try?

Things to practise:

Get into groups of two or more people and compare your usual circles. See whether there is something that someone else in your group is doing that you might want to try.

You could also have people brainstorm a list of activities. At the end, ask folks if there is anything on the list that interests them.

Things to try:

Pick one new thing and, in the next two weeks, give it a try. Afterwards, talk about whether it might be something you would do again.

Also, talk about whether there was anyone there that you could connect with if you decide to go back, or someone from there that you could contact to take part with you in alternate activities.

TIP: By now, the people in your group are probably chomping at the bit to share their own ideas for ways to make friends. Tell them to hold tight, we are more than half way to number 101 – What Might You Do?

Be the kind of friend you'd like to meet (52)

This could well be the most important section in this manual. Because if you are not the kind of person you would like to meet, how can you expect to attract anyone else worth befriending?

Create a vision for yourself as the kind of a person that you would choose to spend time with. If you would choose yourself as a partner, you will be much more likely to be attractive to other people.

And if you are someone who has the traits that other folks are looking for - your chance for friendships increases.

As your network grows, you will find that one of the things that will happen is that the people within your group inspire each other to be better. Friends help us to aspire to more. We've come to think this is one of the most important aspects of relationships.

Alone, we sometimes make plans that we think are good, but they might be just the safest plans. A trusted network of friends might say, "Yeah, but what if you did something slightly different? What if instead of going away for a weekend, you took a cruise for ten days in Europe?" They might make suggestions that help you to be more ambitious for yourself, to expand your horizons. And they'll support you to feel like you can do it!

126

Things to talk about:

Demonstrating a positive attitude is of major importance.

Be the kind of person who always seeks solutions. Don't complain, instead try to be accommodating. As self-advocate leader Barb Goode is fond of saying, "You can catch more flies with honey than with vinegar." In other words, be kind and positive, and treat people the way you want to be treated.

Avoid gossip – don't talk about people behind their backs. Be honest, be loyal, and be respectful.

Be there for your friends in good times and bad.

Questions to discuss:

What traits are you looking for in a friend? Do you exhibit those traits? Are there things you could work on that would make you a more desirable friend?

These can be hard questions to answer honestly. But it is well worth the effort if the result is that you are able to open yourself up to deeper and more meaningful relationships.

Things to practise:

Have folks come up with a list of favourable qualities that they seek in their relationships with others.

Things to try:

In your day-to-day interactions, strive to be the person that you would like to meet. Take note of whether people begin to treat you differently.

A pleasant side-effect is that while you are making yourself more attractive as a friend to others, you could quite possibly become

127

more of a friend to yourself!

TIP: Remember your affirmations!

Sit in a different spot and meet new people (53)

If you always do what you've always done, you'll always get what you've always got.

Things to talk about:

Sitting in a new spot at the game, or at the bar, or at the coffee shop – anywhere, really – opens the door to meeting new people and expanding our personal support networks. You can still keep doing things at the same time and at the same place – just changing this one aspect of your regular activity can lead you to new friendships.

Questions to discuss:

How might things change for the positive if folks do their usual activities, but choose to sit in a different spot?

Things to practise:

Rehearse the introductions and conversation ideas that you came up with in the earlier sections of this book. Or come up with some new ones. You could chat about current events, say hello in another language, or mention a movie or a book that you have recently enjoyed.

Things to try:

The next time you are partaking in one of your regular activities, pick a different spot to sit.

If someone is sitting alone, consider sitting with them.

Not Alone Never Were

Break the ice by introducing yourself and starting a conversation.

Draw others to you (the law of attraction) (54)

Build your own interests so that people have something to ask you about.

Things to talk about:

It seems obvious, but it is well worth saying that it is our variety of interests and our way of talking about them that makes us interesting.

By building our interests, we are a) sure to meet new people, b) always learning new things and c) making ourselves more interesting to others. In essence, we are expanding our horizons!

Questions to discuss:

What are your current interests? (A lot of people discover that they are already more interesting than they previously gave themselves credit.)

What are some interests you have that you have not yet explored?

Things to practise:

Make a list of peoples' current interests and their future interests. Is there anyone in your group whose current interests match, or whose current interest matches someone else's future interests?

129

Perhaps those people could plan a day to get together and talk.

Have folks pair up, preferably with someone new. Take a maximum of ten minutes (up to five minutes each) to ask your partner about what makes them interesting. Remember the listening skills you've learned. Afterwards have a discussion about how people felt talking about their passions with someone else. Ask folks to share a little about what they learned from this experience.

At home, practice talking about your interests with the people in your network.

Things to try:

Sign up for a class! Join a club! Start a club! Pursue your interests and make your self interesting and attractive to others!

Also, be known as a person who always asks others about their interests.

Build your own family tree (55)

Do some research and see who else is out there, waiting for you to call...

It is easy to lose connections with the people we love. Folks from the institutions almost all have relatives they haven't seen for a long time. By studying your family tree you can learn who all your relatives are.

Things to talk about:

One interesting thing that we have been finding while doing

this workshop is that folks interested in their own family history tend to meet others who want to build a family tree – you might end up joining a genealogy club and making new friends with people in the club!

Questions to discuss:

Do you have family members with whom you have lost touch?

Do you have an interest in your ancestry? Maybe you come from a line of royalty! Maybe your great, great grandmother was a women's rights leader!

Things to practise:

Starting is easy. Make a list of family you'd like to reconnect with. Go through the phone book – you might be surprised how easy it is to track them down. Google the names you hope to find – you never know, you could get lucky. Ask your other relatives to help you.

Things to try:

As you discover your relatives' contact information, give them a call and tell them you'd like to see them. You will probably find, like we almost always did, that they are happy you called, and that they would love to get together and be included in your life and your network.

If you ever lived in an institution, you can apply for your files through the freedom of information act. These records often include names and contact information of family members. If you need help with this, ask a trusted person from your network.

Ask whether your local community has a genealogy club. Besides finding relatives and learning about your family's history, these clubs are great places to learn about local history and to meet new people with similar interests.

TIPS: Among many other genealogy on-line resources, Library and Archives Canada hosts the Canadian Genealogy Centre website at www.genealogy.gc.ca. There is also the Canadian Genealogy Resources site at www.canadiangenealogy.net.

Community Centres and Continuing Education Centres sometimes have courses available on how to build your family tree.

Get a Facebook account (56)

...or join some other social networking site.

Love it or hate it, Facebook is a great teacher for those of us wanting to support the development of networks. Everything about Facebook is designed to connect you (or re-connect you) with others. As of this moment, the Facebook FAQ says, there are "[m]ore than 500 million active users," "50% of our active users log on to Facebook in any given day," and the "[a]verage user has 130 friends."

Things to talk about:

It helps to talk first about how social networking websites are an on-line community that is widely diverse. There are millions of people on Facebook looking for new friends who share similar interests. A person can develop friendships with folks from all over the world!

Questions to discuss:

Ask who in your group has a Facebook account. Ask them what they like about it. Ask them how Facebook supports them to deepen their connections and make new friends.

Typical answers might be: Facebook gives you updates on people

132

you may not know well enough to see on a regular basis; Facebook makes friend suggestions based on the friends of your friends; your Facebook friends can also suggest friends; you can join groups on Facebook; Facebook has instant messaging. Even when you can't get out, you can still connect with your friends! Are there any of these things we can do for each other?

Things to practise:

If your group has a computer available, you could open up the Facebook homepage and check out the features. If people want to open an account, the facilitator could assist them, or you could Google 'Facebook video tutorials' and watch short video clips that walk you through the process. You can also create groups on Facebook – perhaps your group would like to do that, and connect with other groups in other places?

Things to try:

Sign up and start searching for friends. Facebook has a few tools to assist you in this. It's easiest if people look at these with someone who has tried some of them.

TIPS: For an interesting alternative to Facebook, check out www.tyze.com. Tyze is an on-line social site specifically to connect folks with their networks. It was developed by the Planned Lifetime Advocacy Network (PLAN) and has a unique set of tools to allow everyone in your network to be involved and to track and celebrate successes. Find out more about the Planned Lifetime Advocacy Network at www.planinstitute.com. Another interesting site to help you develop a network is www.lotsahelpinghands.com

Take a workshop on internet safety (57)

This section should be paired with Number 56 – Get a Facebook account.

It is important to learn how to safely share your information online. There definitely are safety issues to be aware of, such as identity theft, viruses, and fraud, among others.

There are privacy settings on Facebook and other social networking sites that are important to learn about.

Things to talk about:

Our friend Gary was doing a lot of tutoring, and he gave an internet safety course for people with disabilities. He got participants to brain-storm a list of all the things that you should never do on the internet. They came up with a really good list.

Then he asked them whether they agreed that they shouldn't ever do any of those things – and everyone put up their hands. Next, he said "So, if you have never done any of these things you can put your hand down." Only three out of fifty participants lowered their hands.

Facilitators should take this opportunity to talk about general internet safety. This would also be a good time to talk specifically about on-line social network privacy issues and settings.

Internet safety should be an ongoing conversation for us all.

Questions to discuss:

Ask the folks in your group who already have a Facebook account whether they have ever taken an internet safety course. If so, they could tell the rest of the group what they learned and how to sign up.

Things to practise:

To find an internet safety course, look in your community centre course guide and your local adult education guide. Alternatively, ask at your community centre or at your community police office about course availability in your area. Often, the police will have information about internet safety; they may even be able to offer to teach a group about internet safety issues.

Things to try:

Look for upcoming internet safety courses and sign up for the next one.

TIPS: Google 'internet safety tips'. You will get a lot of kids' sites, but these can be helpful too. Add the word 'adult' to your search to narrow down the results.

If there are no internet safety courses available in your community, ask whether there is anyone within your agency who could share their knowledge on this important subject. Suggest to your community centre or police office that they consider providing a course.

Practice asking people for their phone number (58)

Things to talk about:

Asking people for their phone number is a great social cue – you're letting folks know that you're interested in them in a way that doesn't put too much pressure on them. Yet, in our very first workshop more than ten years ago, it turned out that the staff helpers found this harder to do than the folks who were (intentional) participants.

Questions to discuss:

135

How does it make you feel to have someone you like ask you for your phone number?

Do you always make sure to have your address book handy, so that you can add the phone numbers you have asked for right away?

Things to practice:

You will want to practice this; most of us do not know how to ask for a phone number. What we have found in our workshops is that people with disabilities are often better at this than their staff are. Facilitators, here is an opportunity to let people with disabilities teach.

Ask your group for volunteers to role play asking for phone numbers.

For this section, it is great if people have come prepared with their address books, or if you have address books to hand out.

Things to try:

Folks within your group could ask each other for their phone numbers and add them to their address books right away.

When you are out in your community, ask someone you see regularly for their phone number.

Have friends' phone numbers and email addresses handy – reminds you to stay in touch (59)

Some people carry a paper address book; others have their contact information stored in their cell phone memory; other people use their computers, or the margins of the family calendar. There are a number of ways to store contacts, but the most important thing is that it belongs to the person and is easy to access.

Besides your address book, you might also want to keep a list of your closest friends and relatives near the phone.

Things to talk about:

Talk about having a useful address book that can be carried with you all the time: what might this lead to?

What Will You Celebrate Today?

Some ideas – it reminds you to keep in touch. It gives you a way to document new friends you meet.

Questions to discuss:

What kind of address book suits you? Ask people in your group to share their systems with the others.

Do you have a list of close contacts on your fridge door, or hanging up near your phone? Is it the same list or a different one? Why?

Things to practice:

Get people to find the contact information for their friends and family. Discuss whether the information was truly handy or not. Talk about ways to make the information more accessible.

Like all of these ideas, this should never lead to feeling badly for

137

anyone – if folks don't have any contact information, or if their information wasn't easily accessible, that's okay. The goal is simply to get folks thinking about a system that will really work for them.

The idea is to find the handiest, easiest, most ownable way to consistently stay in touch!

Things to try:

Really inexpensive address books are available at dollar stores, or you can print out a one page example with a few phone numbers on it to get people started. Once, after a workshop, someone in the U.S. came up and said "Great idea! I've just called back to the office and ordered address books for *all* our folks! We support 1000 people!" Wow! One small step towards person-centredness!

Have a phone that works for you (60)

John's family was frustrated because he never returned their calls. This had been an issue for years, but everyone in the family felt uncomfortable talking about it.

It turned out he couldn't punch in the numbers – his fingers are too big for a regular push button telephone. He was embarrassed to talk about it, and so the misunderstandings grew and grew as they left calls and he didn't call back. Luckily, someone noticed the problem and suggested a phone designed for people with sight difficulties – a phone with really big numbers, and with handy speed-dial settings. Now he returns his calls and has regular phone conversations with the people in his network. This one thing significantly changed everything for his network, not least because they realised it wasn't that he didn't want to talk to them.

Things to talk about:

Have a discussion about how an adaptation can help people to have

138

more independence. Talk about how many people use many different devices to help them communicate.

Some of the adaptive features you can get are phones that couple with hearing aids or computers, phones with easy grip handsets, or hands-free capability, or visual ringing signals, among many others.

Questions to discuss:

Are there features you wish you had on your phone? Chances are that they are available.

Things to practice:

Call your telephone service provider and ask about adaptive devices or programs that you might be able to get. You might also call your local hearing clinic, or in a larger city they sometimes have centres for people who are deaf or hard of hearing where they advise you on aids and can lend you things to test.

Go and look at telephones for sale – you may see just the right one for you.

Things to try:

Now you've got the phone with the features you need – start catching up on your calls!

Have a supply of personalized business cards (61)

Things to talk about:

Besides being a great way to share your contact information, this idea can be used as a way to redirecting challenging behaviours. Mishel and Jesse work with a fellow named Rex, who has the unfortunate behaviour of giving people an underhand smack on the behind. Mishel and Jesse came up with the idea of business cards,

139

because it allowed Rex to put his underhand smacking movement to better use. Now, instead of smacking people, he has a business card ready to hand off to them.

Often people just need a way to enter a conversation!

However, it also worked for other people as an easy way to carry contact information, which they can then transfer into their address books. Business cards also have a way of making folks feel important, and since you are important, why not feel important!

There are many business card printing programs available for the computer, and sheets of printable cards are available at any stationary store for reasonable prices. Some brands of printable business cards even come with card printing software included. One group of folks took this idea and built on it by adding photos of each group member to their cards. Another great idea!

Questions to discuss:

Would you like to have your own business cards?

What information would you want to give out? Some people might want more than one kind of card. For example, one card might include your address, and another might not. Perhaps you want some people to only get your email address and others your telephone number. If people are non-verbal, they might want a card that simply says, "Hi, my name is Rex. What's your name?" The DIY printing makes it very flexible.

Things to practice:

Print up a few cards on the computer. If people don't have access to a computer, perhaps a volunteer or family member can assist them?

Things to try:

Give out cards to people you'd like to see again.

TIP: You could also get fridge magnets made with your name and contact information on them. You could even put a photo of yourself on them to remind people who you are. Our friend Jack did this when he moved from one place to another, as a way of reminding his friends he was still around, just in a new place!

Connect with your past (62)

We've already talked about the idea of connecting with old friends, and the experiment we did around re-connection in which only one person didn't want to get together. It was no ones intention to distance themselves, but things "just happened."

In this exercise you might want to focus more on that idea, or you might want to talk about the idea that all of us have a story – we come out of a series of events and become who we are. How do people get opportunities to tell their stories? Do they know how?

Questions to discuss:

What's important to you? What's a story that focuses on that idea? What five ideas could you put together that might help you tell this story? For example, share the point the story will be making. Then tell the story in three parts. Then confirm the point of the story.

  1) the point of the story: "The thing about me is that I always love to be around dogs, and I always have. This is a story about a dog that I loved."

The story 2) "I got a puppy from the S.P.C.A. and then I realized she was deaf. Everyone had thought she was just a brat."

The story 3) "I had to learn sign language to communicate with her, and she was so happy to be able to know what I wanted."

The story 4) "After that I taught her how to watch my hands and I could give her hand signals when no one was watching. Everyone thought she was the world's smartest dog then!"

The point of the story 5) "That experience with my deaf dog taught me a lot. Now, when I meet someone who seems to be having some trouble, I wonder if we're really understanding how they communicate? What do we need to learn to make sure that things work for them?"

Things to practice:

What's a story people might want to tell? Discuss when having a story to share would be a good thing.   What can we learn from each others' stories?

Organize a "girls' night out" or a "boys night out" (63)

L'Arche Foundation on Vancouver Island host breakfasts on the weekends. They have a boys' breakfast and a girls' breakfast – it's an activity everyone looks forward to.   Something in common, simply stated ("we're all girls") can lead to closer connections ("we're all girls who like karaoke – let's get together every month").

Neighbourly

Things to talk about:

Think about your friends of the same gender. Do you do things together as a group? If not, could you?

A lot of people think of a night out with the girls/boys as a night at the pub, but you can do anything you like. Have themes like French night. Pick a French restaurant, learn a couple of French phrases, or go to a French movie with subtitles. You get the idea.

Or make each night out a trip down memory lane. Each time, a different person in your group gets to pick activities or places that have a special significance for them. This is a great way to get to know your friends on a deeper level.

Another part of this that can be useful is to have each participant organize the event: they can figure out how much it will cost everyone to practice budgeting, figure out the transit that will get people there, figure out the timing by doing some research.

Questions to discuss:

If you were to invite your boys or girls group to go out, where could you go? Think in terms of common interests, but be open to trying new things too.

Things to practice:

Come up with a list of ideas for boys'/girls' nights out. Be creative with your list, but try to pick something that everyone will enjoy. If you're not sure what everyone likes, give them a call and ask them for their input.

Things to try:

Call up the girls/boys in your network and invite them out. Once again – be the person in your network that brings people together to have fun!

Send postcards to people when you go traveling – powerful experience – people love post cards (64)

Things to talk about:

Don't you love getting post cards? We don't know anyone who doesn't have a special place in their heart for people who remember to send them post card greetings from abroad. It is a meaningful thing for people and can lead to deeper relationships.

Almost everyone who receives a post card will put it up on their fridge, or some other special place, as a memento of their friendship.

Questions to discuss:

Why do you suppose people love getting post cards?

What would you write on a post card to a friend?

Things to practice:

A really good facilitator we met does an ice-breaker where she has collected a lot of post-cards and each person has to pick their favourite and their least favourite. Breaking into small groups, they explain their choices. Often people will get to know each other better just by doing this.

Practice writing short greetings to friends. If writing is a challenge, have someone help write a quick message and the person's address on the card for you. Perhaps you could get a rubber stamp made that says "thinking of you." Or "wish you were here." Or you could collect stickers from your holiday spot and stick those onto the back of the post card along with your signature. You could bring along your friends' addresses pre-printed on peel-and-stick labels.

Things to try:

Next time you go on a trip somewhere, remember to bring your address book. Pick up a few post cards and some stamps and start writing.

Not going away? Buy art post cards or any interesting post cards from your own home town and send those. Collect nice post cards that you can send anytime!

Compliment someone on something you've noticed about them - try complimenting someone in the room right now (65)

Things to talk about:

Compliments lift the hearts of the recipients and make them feel good about themselves. They lift our spirits; both giver and receiver. They are another way to celebrate success. A compliment about someone's appearance, or something they have done or created, shows people that you care about them.

Questions to discuss:

How do compliments make you feel?

If you come from a family or a setting where compliments were unusual or even non-existent, giving them might not come naturally to you at first. If you're nervous about giving compliments, what can you do to make it easier?

Things to practice:

Make a point to notice nice things about people. Start by complimenting people within your network. Once you get used to giving compliments, it becomes easier and easier.

Of course, compliments must be sincere. A sincere compliment is heartfelt and honest. In other words, don't say something if you don't mean it.

Try this: break up into small groups and take turns giving each of

145

the folks within your group a sincere compliment.

Doesn't it make you feel good to get one? And doesn't it feel good to give them?

When you become a person who is known for giving sincere compliments, the people around you will feel closer to you, and you will feel closer to yourself.

Things to try:

When you're out, if you notice something nice about someone, give the person a compliment. Take note of their reaction. Take note, too, about how it makes you feel.

Next time you're at a meeting with your entire support network, give each person a list with the names of everyone there, with enough space between each name for everyone to write down a sincere compliment for each of the other people on the list. Then compile the compliments for each individual in the group. Give each person their list of compliments to keep. We know folks who did these kinds of lists when they were in elementary school, and they have kept their list in a special place ever since.

Doing this exercise, we sometimes find out that people we thought might not like us really do!

TIP: Add this to your list of affirmations: "I am a person who makes others feel good by giving compliments!"

By the way, when you get a compliment, it is important not to discount or dismiss it. Accept compliments graciously and make the giver feel good about their kindness.

Get your staff to step back so others can step in; staff want to be perceived to be useful, but this can get in the way (66)

146

Place your own order at the coffee shop. Accept help from another customer instead of having your staff do everything.

Things to talk about:

Staff often assume that their job is to help with everything. They need to be made to feel okay about stepping back.

It is important for people to have a staff team who all know when to step back and allow natural supports the chance to grow. It's important that people know about ideas like learned helplessness and how they can build on independence. Make sure your staff feel supported in this endeavour by their co-workers and their agency.

Questions to discuss:

How do we make our staff feel okay about stepping back?

How can staff and their agencies make people being supported feel okay about asking their staff to step back?

Things to practice:

Talk to everyone in your network and let them know that you want to develop natural supports and relationships with unpaid others, and that there are times when you will need your staff to step back to allow this to occur.

Role play asking staff nicely to step back. You might even develop a signal or a polite look you can give, so that your staff will know when to step back without having to be asked verbally.

As you gain confidence with this, you should eventually see your staff intuitively stepping back without needing any cues. In fact, we believe that fading support like this is one of the most important skills for staff to learn.

Things to try:

Next time you're out with staff and there is a chance for natural support to replace paid support, ask your staff to step back. Since you've talked to your network about this and practiced with your staff beforehand, this should not be a feel-bad experience. Quite the opposite; you might just develop a relationship with someone new. And that feels great!

Talk about pets (67)

If you don't have any pets, ask people about theirs – it's simple and not too personal and it can lead to other conversations

Things to talk about:

In our workshops, when we talk about personal networks 100% of people want to talk about pets. The couple of times we've forgotten to talk about pets, folks brought it up with some urgency.

In one of our workshops, we asked everyone to have a short conversation with a person they didn't know and then introduce them to the rest of the group. (By the way, this in itself is a great way to meet new people.) Anyway, every single introduction included comments about pets.

Pets give you something in common and give you places to meet – the pet food store, the dog park, the cat show, the animal shelter....

Questions to discuss:

Do you have any good pet stories?

Do you stop to talk to your neighbours about their pets? If not, definitely try this. People love to talk about their pets.

Would you like to have a pet, or offer to look after your friends' pets?

Discuss how some people like pets that other people wouldn't want in their homes. Spiders for example. Or birds, for some people. What does this teach us about diversity?

Things to practice:

Think of the people you know who have pets. Practice starting a conversation about their dog, cat, bird, snake, ferret, rat, iguana....

Things to try:

Go out and talk to people about their pets! The next time you see someone with their pet, say hello and start a pet conversation.

Volunteer to walk dogs or care for the animals at your local animal shelter. This can be a great way to meet new friends and to do something for your community. It's also a great way to see whether pet ownership is for you. It is wise to think about the responsibility and expense of pet ownership before you decide to get one, and volunteering at the S.P.C.A. is a smart first step in figuring that out.

Camping

Organize a camping trip (68)

There's nothing like shared holiday memories of sticky "s'mores" in the rain to cement a relationship. Camping can be an intense social experience and shared memories of the fun you had can last a lifetime.

149

For some folks, it is their only way to get away from technology and the kinds of assumptions about life that happen in a city.

Things to talk about:

Have folks share some of their best (or worst!) camping experiences.

If you're thinking about going camping for the first time, have a discussion about what you would need to bring with you.

Questions to discuss:

Do you like camping, or the idea of camping?

Would you sleep in a tent, or are you more of a cabin or camper person?

Do you have all the equipment you'll need for a camping trip, or a friend you could borrow some equipment from?

How long would you want to be away?

Things to practice:

Things to try:

Pick a nice spot, invite your friends, go and set up your camper or pitch your tent, and have fun!

Say hello to your camping neighbours. Invite them over for a cup of campfire coffee or a toasted marshmallow.

"Thus we take charge of the state of our lives and become an active agent in defining who we are and what we would like to be. Though this will not ensure that we do not fall short, it will nonetheless contribute to our further development towards being the kind of person who is sincere in being good when it matters. Reflections on values that challenge us and those that do not"

Michael J. Kendrick PhD

TIP: Google camping in 'my Province'. In British Columbia, where we live, www.camping.bc.ca has a list of every campground in the Province and special rates for folks with disabilities.

Shop locally (69)

Our friend Anne Marie suggests getting to know the stores in your neighbourhood or going to the farmer's market.

Instead of going out to the mall or to the super grocery store, try shopping in your own neighbourhood. Support the businesses of your neighbours, and they will remember you.

Farmer's markets attract lots of locals and they are great places to meet your neighbours. You can often get things that you can't find anywhere else. If you are into growing vegetables, or arts and crafts, or baking, or any other market enterprise, you could consider renting a table yourself.

Things to talk about:

Busy neighbourhood businesses make an area vibrant and fun. And increased pedestrian traffic makes the neighbourhood safer for everyone.

Questions to discuss:

Are there some interesting businesses in your community?

Are there any restaurants in your neighbourhood that you haven't tried yet?

Things to practice:

Look in your community newspapers to learn more about the businesses in your neighbourhood. Maybe you will come across some articles or advertisements, some coupons or some restaurant two-for-one offers.

Find out if there is a farmer's market in your community and where and when it takes place.

Things to try:

Go out and buy your fruit and vegetables from the local farmer's market. Say hello to your neighbours.

Invite a friend to try out a new café or restaurant. Check out the pet store, the hair salon, the hardware store...

Go to the movie everyone is talking about – things in common – start meetings with this topic to get out of business mode (70)

Free 2

Make it a point to go to the movie that everyone is talking about. One of our friends, James, always does this.

James kept finding that everyone was in a rush: "Okay, we have this limited amount of time and there are these important issue, so let's talk about them and get this over with." Which meant no one was getting to know each other, and often he wondered if that wasn't more important than the things they thought were important. How could he expect his team of staff to priorise relationships for those they supported if they weren't able to model doing it for themselves?

James suggested that they try starting meetings with, "So, how is everyone doing?" But some people couldn't imagine being so casual at a meeting.

Next, James took some leadership by going to see whatever was the most popular movie, so he could begin with, "So, what about that new blockbuster movie!? Did anyone see it?" Suddenly everyone wanted to talk about movies at the meetings, and just as much work got done. The tone of the meetings improved. People who had experienced being listened to felt more inclined to contribute positively to the agenda. There was an increased tendency to talk about things like relationships and to keep things optimistic.

Some people started seeing movies just to have something to discuss at their meetings.

Things to talk about:

Ask the folks in your group whether they have seen any movies lately, then stand back and watch the conversations erupt.

Movies are entertaining and they give us something in common with many other people.

Questions to discuss:

Have a discussion with your group about why movies are such great conversation starters. Why do you suppose people like to talk about movies?

Are there any movie clubs in your community? If not, think about starting one. One of our friends started going to a "meet-up" movie group where he quickly became one of the people everyone wanted to talk to because he knew so much about movies!

Things to practice:

Rehearse a movie conversation you might have with someone. Go to the movies, or rent some DVD's. Prepare yourself to make movie friends.

Things to try:

The next time you have the chance; ask someone whether they have seen the movie everyone is talking about. The more people you ask, the better chance of finding someone who shares your movie interests!

Be a neighbourhood trick-or-treat stop at Hallowe'en (71)

Our friend Bryan collects things all year long to prepare for Halloween – everyone knows him for this.

People remember Bryan from year to year for his Hallowe'en creativity. Bryan has limited social skills, but that doesn't deter his friends and neighbours from stopping all throughout the year to say hello and to find out what he's planning to do for the next Hallowe'en. Sometimes Bryan likes to signal "Ssshhh!" and grin, to let them know it's a big secret. Everyone enjoys this.

> "The more I think it over, the more I feel that there is nothing more truly artistic than to love people."
>
> **Vincent van Gogh**

Things to talk about:

Hallowe'en is a very popular family event. What do people like about it?

Questions to discuss:

Does your neighbourhood celebrate at Hallowe'en? Do you celebrate? How many kids are in your neighbourhood? Does your local community centre sponsor Hallowe'en events like pumpkin carving, haunted houses, scavenger hunts, or costume parties?

154

Are you prepared with everything you'll need for next Hallowe'en?

Things to practice:

Think about how you might decorate your yard. Think about how to make your home attractive and safe (but also scary) for trick-or-treaters. You can collect what you need all throughout the year.

Things to try:

On Hallowe'en night play scary music and dress up in your costume. Have enough goodies ready to hand out to the kids. Become the house that kids from all over your neighbourhood remember as a fun Hallowe'en haunt.

Invite friends over for a costume party or to stay up late watching scary movies.

Communicate as clearly and confidently as you can (72)

Our friend April got rid of all her complicated communications systems - and there were many different ones. She found that the people who know and love her can understand her without the complex, high-tech communication devices that kept breaking down and required so much support. And those people can help April to communicate with others. Thus, she created an easier system for herself – a clear system that she is more confident about, which depends on relationships - and she has never looked back. She keeps everyone's photographs and phone numbers and a selection of photos of things she's been doing that she wants to talk about.

> **"You don't have to get it right the first time."**
>
> **Barbara Sher**

Many folks have created simple communication systems that depend on ready access to information that is important to them.

155

If you have an augmentative communication system, include important names, places and events so you can talk about the things that matter to you.

Things to talk about:

Some of the clearest communicators we know are self advocates.

Confident communication is about being honest, open, and clear. Some characteristics of confidence in communication are direct eye contact, welcoming body language, and a tone that is assertive without being intimidating. Use gestures and facial expressions in a way that will enhance your conversations and promote better understanding.

Confident communication helps put our listeners at ease.

Some other benefits to being confident are: increased self-esteem; deeper relationships; and decreased chance of misunderstanding. If you are confident, your friends will become more confident. It really is true that we are known by the company we keep.

One of the key components to clear communication is taking the time to figure out how the person you are communicating with understands best. And, of course, no one should ever be afraid to ask for clarification if something is said that is not understood.

Questions to discuss:

Is there anyone in your group who is known for their clear and confident communication style? Ask them for some pointers.

Things to practice:

Split your group up into pairs. Have each pair pick a topic of conversation – like pets for example – and practice being clear and confident. Take turns being the speaker and the listener. At the end have a discussion about how it went for people.

Things to try:

In every interaction you have, try to be conscious of your clarity and your confidence level. Think of confidence-building as an ongoing, life-long process.

TIP: If a lack of confidence seems to be an insurmountable problem for you, consider talking to someone about it. There is no shame in asking for support.

Be a good listener (73)

We've been really surprised to come to understand, repeatedly, about how important the power of listening is. This is our main theme for our agency's services, and not one we would have predicted. While we kept thinking people wanted other things from us, they kept saying "and the best thing is that you really listened to me." This made us wonder how to do better what we already do well, and we are constantly, consciously trying to learn how to be better listeners.

> "A purpose of human life, no matter who is controlling it, is to love whoever is around to be loved."
>
> **Kurt Vonnegut**

Things to talk about:

A good listener makes the people they communicate with feel important. Also, if you listen well, you can learn things about folks that could deepen your relationships with them. If you learn to be a person who listens, you will find that other people listen more closely to you as well.

Barb Goode, a world-renowned self advocate, would remind us at this point that it is equally important to listen to folks who are non-verbal, seeing that talking is just one of many forms of

157

communication. Barb says that non-verbal people (and others) speak volumes with their eyes, their facial expressions, and their body language - and even with their behaviours.

If people are a little introverted, this is their time to shine. You see, introverts are generally really good listeners. They are more prone to think before they speak, and they try to see things from the other person's perspective – and these are important skills for all listeners to develop.

Questions to ask:

Ask yourself, "Am I a good listener?" Be honest with yourself. Many people could be better listeners – the point here is to start working on it, then keep focusing on improvement. This should be an ongoing process wherein you continuously re-evaluate your progress.

Rock

Things to practice:

Break up into groups of two or three. Pick a topic and practice your listening skills. Take turns being the speaker and the listener.

Then, have a discussion about how it feels to have people really listen to you.

Things to try:

From this point on keep a focus on honing your listening skills. In every conversation you have, try to make sure your partner feels that what they have to say is worth listening to.

Join a community choir (74)

Dying in the community is one of the stages of living in the community. Funerals are a right of passage, as important as any other. At a funeral we went to for a much-loved community member, four choirs sang. She had been a member of all of them and about half the mourners were people she had sung with somewhere, somehow. It was an enviable celebration of her life.

Things to talk about:

People who sing often become more outgoing. Their creativity improves and they tend to become more successful in other areas of their lives. Educators believe that students who join choirs end up better connected to their communities.

Questions to discuss:

Do you like to sing? Have you ever thought of joining a choir?

Do you sing along to your favourite bands, or sing in the shower?

Things to practice:

Look into community or church choirs in your area – they are often looking for new members. Most places have a choral federation, whose goal is to connect people with choirs in their area.

Things to try:

Sing a song!

Pick a choir to join and go try out! You'll find that choral singers are very supportive of each other. This is a fantastic way to build meaningful relationships with others who share your passion for singing.

Collect something, and talk to others who share your passion

(75)

Many people collect things. Jim collects a lot of different things, but books are his main passion. As a book collector, he has relationships with several used book store owners and staff. He also attends collector's meetings and used book sales. The library has seminars on collecting and holds sales a few times a year, where, if he's lucky, he might just find one of the elusive collectible books he has been searching for. At all these locations and events he sees people he knows, and they always have interesting conversations about their passion for books.

Things to talk about:

Mildred started off collecting Elvis records and memorabilia. She had friends who were interested enough to go along with her on her

The Cat Who Was Home Everywhere He Went

collecting jaunts, and some of them became passionate Elvis collectors too, and then they met passionate Elvis collectors who became friends. These folks ended up starting a group to support her to live independently. What started off being about Elvis became a network of caring friends who happened to have a shared passion.

Collecting is more than just buying stuff. People collect all kinds of things, but for the purposes of relationship building, collecting is more about becoming connected to a group of folks with the same

160

passions as you. If you are just starting out, you might want to ask around at Antique or Collectibles stores to see if there are any groups of collectors in your area.

You might want to pick items to collect based on groups in your community that have regular meetings.

Questions to discuss:

Ask for a show of hands to find out who the collectors are in your group. What do they collect? Are there collectors clubs that they belong to? Maybe some of the folks who are not yet collectors might want to join a club that someone else in the group belongs to. Or if there are people in your group with similar interests, they might want to start a club of their own.

Things to practice:

Find out what collectors clubs there are in your community. Find out when and where they meet and go to the next meeting. Check a meeting out first to decide whether it is the right collecting club for you. Be open-minded. For instance, an aquarium society or an specialty garden club are forms of collectors clubs.

Alternately, find out if anyone you already know is a collector. Ask them if you can tag along with them next time they go out collecting. If you like it, but there are no clubs to join, suggest starting a club with them.

Things to try:

To avoid filling your home up too quickly, try being more specific with your collection. For example, instead of collecting any old salt and pepper shakers, just collect shakers in the shape of animals, or Depression glass shakers, or wooden shakers, or whatever – it's up to you.

161

Now go out and start collecting. Become a regular in your local thrift shops, flea markets, and antique stores. Check out yard sales (another great way to get to know your neighbours). Go to your collectors' meetings and chat with others about your cool finds.

TIP: Google collector's clubs 'my town'. We were surprised at the number of clubs and the range of collectibles in our town. The first page alone had local gatherings for collectors of dolls, historical cameras, pins, cars, pens, model railroads, and corkscrews. The list is literally endless. Michael Kendrick once said to us, "It turns out that if you're interested in something – no matter how odd it might seem to others – you will find you're not the only one and someone will want to talk about it. Isn't that remarkable?" Corkscrews?

Show an interest in what others are saying (76)

We have found that people sometimes need to role play this level of empathy. People with and without disabilities very often find it hard to consistently look interested in what others are saying.

Always remember, no life is insignificant and no story is without its value.

Things to talk about:

To help you focus on showing an interest when you are with someone, try to see, hear and feel the meaning of what they are telling you.

Showing true empathy shows that you identify with someone else's feelings. It makes you a better friend and increases your chances for deeper relationships.

Questions to discuss:

Are you a good listener? Do you make a point to look interested in

162

what people are saying to you?

How does it make us feel when people are truly interested in our opinions?

Have you ever had a conversation with someone who looks bored or lacks empathy? Have you experienced interactions with people who seemed to show no interest in your conversation? How does that lack of interest make you feel?

Things to practice:

Take plenty of opportunities to role play showing an interest in conversations. Pretend there is a video camera taping all your interactions. If you played it back, how would you come across? It is actually quite easy to set up a camera and watch yourself "listening" and see what impression you are making and what you might want to change.

Practice "active listening" whereby you maintain eye contact and show through your facial expressions and your body language that you are interested in what your partners are saying.

Notice what someone else is good at and ask them about it (77)

Look for opportunities to give people positive feedback about the things they are good at. This is not as common as it should be, so people take notice when someone takes the time to ask them about their passions.

Things to talk about:

People love to be complimented about the things they're good at. It is a great way to connect more deeply with them; to find out more about their interests. If someone has a great garden, for example, tell them so and ask them questions about it.

Questions to discuss:

How does it make you feel to have someone acknowledge the things that you are good at?

How does it make you feel to give positive feedback? It's a win-win situation!

Things to practice:

Start taking notice of the things that the people around you are good at. Perhaps you have a neighbour with a beautifully-kept aquarium, or a friend who excels at making others feel welcomed - someone you know from the church choir with a wonderful voice, or a co-worker who is an expert at the public transportation system.

Things to try:

Start complimenting folks on the things they're good at! Let them know that you have are interested in them. As a positive side effect, you might notice yourself getting more compliments about the things that you are good at.

Get a job (78)

While this is it's own huge topic, it's also part of life. Self-advocates who have had jobs always have a different sense of who their friends are and who they can rely on than those who have not. And self-advocates who have a job are loathe to go back to not having a job.

For people who have worked somewhere for more than a year or two, co-workers often become their most important circle of support.

For most of us, work is where we have the greatest chance of meeting people and building close friendships, so it shouldn't be a

164

surprise that this is also true for folks with disabilities.

Things to talk about:

Work is a major part of most peoples' identities. We see our co-workers regularly and we often have and become role models on the job. We are constantly learning new skills.

Jobs make us feel empowered and included. We earn money and feel more self-sufficient. When we work we contribute to society in numerous ways.

Yet people with disabilities are drastically under-employed. It is said that, worldwide, more than 80% of people with disabilities live below the poverty line.

Questions to discuss:

How many people in your group are working? Have a discussion about what kinds of jobs they have.

Do folks feel fulfilled in their work? Are their co-workers an important part of their social lives?

For folks with jobs, how would they say that paid work in the community differs from a day program or sheltered workshop?

Remember, most of us get our jobs through our networks and other connections, and so don't forget to ask your friends and other supporters whether they know of any jobs that might be suitable for you.

Things to try:

Start dropping off your résumés and applying for jobs. Don't let a few rejections get you down. Most people apply for several jobs before they are hired. The average seems to be about eight interviews before landing a job, so don't lose hope. Add this to your list of affirmations: "I am an excellent employee!"

Be an advocate or sign up with an advocacy agency to mentor someone (79)

Sometimes it is easier to make sure someone else is heard than to speak up for yourself. But one thing leads to another...

It's all about giving people opportunities for leadership. We all have gifts to share with the world.

Things to talk about:

In this field, when we talk about advocacy agencies, we instantly think of community living agencies, and you certainly could sign up with a community living agency to be an advocate or a mentor. But there are all kinds of advocacy opportunities out there.

There are transit advocacy groups, bicycle safety groups, affordable housing groups, immigrant service groups, human rights groups, animal rights groups, and many more.

This is a great way to share your knowledge and meet folks who care about the same things you do.

Questions to discuss:

Think about your favourite teacher. Wouldn't it be nice to be that favourite teacher for someone else?

What are your passions? What do you want to stand up for? If you're having trouble finding something, ask your staff or your agency to help you.

Things to practice:

> "Restorative community is created when we allow ourselves to use the language of healing and relatedness and belonging without embarrassment. it recognizes that taking responsibility for one's own part in creating the present situation is the critical act of courage and engagement, which is the axis around which the future rotates. The essence of restorative community building is not economic prosperity or the political discourse or the capacity of leadership; it is the citizens' willingness to own up to their contribution, to be humble, to choose accountability, and to have faith in their own capacity to make authentic promises to create the alternative future."
>
> **Peter Block,**
>
> *Community: Structures for Belonging*

Now that you know about some advocacy groups in your community, call or go in to find out more about what they do and how you could fit in. Find out when they meet.

Things to try:

Go to a meeting. Become an advocate. Become a mentor. Speak up for yourself and for others who may not be able to speak for themselves.

TIP: Affirmation: I am a teacher and a social reformer!

Gather people who all want to expand their social lives or social skills (80)

Get everyone you know who wants to expand their social networks and build their social skills to gather together. After all, you already have those goals in common.

Things to talk about:

If you work together with others you are likely to have more and better ideas than you might have on your own.

Questions to discuss:

Who in your group is looking to increase their social networks or to expand on their social skills? (We assume everyone.)

Brainstorm a list of the possible benefits to forming a social focus group.

Things to practice:

Have all the folks in your group who are looking to build their networks and their networking skills discuss the possibility of getting together to talk about how it is going for them. Pick a meeting day and time. Later, invite other people you know who are also building their networks.

Prepare for the meeting by thinking about what kind of social network you want for yourself. Also think about any progress you have made in that regard, or any advice that you might want to share.

Consider making this a regular meeting where people can come to share their stories and ideas about friendship. These meetings themselves become part of your social network. You could make life-long friends with people from this group!

Things to try:

Have your first meeting. If it all goes well, why not suggest to the group that you meet regularly? Pick a time that works for everyone and schedule your next meeting. Maybe the meeting about how to make some new friends will become a meeting of new friends!

Learn to lead (81)

The most powerful and dedicated personal support networks are the ones that are "managed" by the person with a disability themselves – if they have the right supports the degree of disability doesn't seem to matter.

Verbal or non-verbal, lots of staff or no staff, folks who are in charge of their own networks tend to have the strongest support.

Things to talk about:

Who better to decide what they want from their lives than the people themselves. Yet, many folks with disabilities have no control over issues that matter to them. There are still many people with disabilities have never had any opportunity to make any choices – ever.

Questions to discuss:

Are there any people in your group who already manage their own networks? If so, ask them how they would feel about going back to having someone else manage it for them. Ask them why they want to lead their own network.

Ask the people without disabilities in your group how they would feel about handing over the management of their networks to someone else.

How can we best help the people we support to lead their own networks? Hint: don't over-think this and turn it into a 'program'. Think in terms of how we all manage our own lives. We choose our own friends and our own risks, we choose when to have private time, and we do the things that make us happiest in life. In short, we all make our own rules.

Things to practice:

Have regular conversations about how folks can manage their own

169

networks and take on more leadership responsibilities in their lives. Brainstorm a list of ideas at your next meeting.

Think about inviting a self advocate leader to come and talk about how they developed their leadership skills.

Things to try:

Learn to lead. Start slowly. Decide what kind of life you want for yourself and ask the folks in your network for as much help as you need to achieve your goals.

As you take on more leadership roles and become the "manager" of your own network, watch yourself blossom into the person you've always wanted to be.

TIP: Remember, many of the folks at the centre of our networks have never been offered the chance to lead. They will need strong support and plenty of encouragement.

Give yourself permission to miss the mark (82)

Nothing is going to be perfect the first time – to make one friend we need to meet a whole lot of people who won't be our friends.

Things to talk about:

Just keep trying. Many of us are our own worst enemies. We believe that if someone doesn't want to be our friend that there is something wrong with us. In reality people have an infinite number of reasons for their friendship decisions that we have no control over and that in fact have nothing to do with us.

Questions to discuss:

What are some external (outside of ourselves) reasons that someone might have for not wanting to be friends?

Free 3

Things to practice:

Repeat this affirmation: "I am ready for the right friend for me."

Keep practising what you have learned about making friends, and if you're ever feeling discouraged, talk it over with the people in your network.

Things to try:

Keep putting yourself out there. Using the ideas you have learned in this book, go out and continue meeting new people. If it takes time, it will definitely be time well spent!

Practise introducing yourself to new people (83)

Things to talk about:

Many self advocates are great at this. They are often better than anyone at introducing themselves to new people.

This can be difficult for a lot of us, but it doesn't have to be. Just practice a simple introduction until you feel confident. Some pointers: make eye contact; smile; don't be afraid to throw in some humour. A short, firm (but not bone-crushing) handshake tells the person you are confident.

Questions to discuss:

Are there any people in your group who are experts at the art of

171

self-introduction? Maybe they can share some of their skills with the others.

Have a discussion about what might make folks nervous about introducing themselves, and then brainstorm a list of suggestions to make it easier for them.

Things to practice:

Rehearse your introduction with people in your network. Keep it simple and be clear and confident. Personally, I would start with, "Hello, my name is Jim."

Things to try:

The next time you have the chance to introduce yourself to a new person, do it! When you see how easy it really is, you'll become more relaxed and ready to do it the next time. When you see the positive responses you get, it will make you feel great about yourself.

TIP: Google 'How to introduce yourself' for lots of introduction pointers for use in casual and professional situations.

Stay hopeful (84)

In one of our very first workshops we realized that a major issue for people was that they had lost hope. Folks and families had lost hope that there was anyone they could rely on and that there were people who would be accountable. They had lost hope that anyone would want to befriend the person at the centre of the network.

Things to talk about:

Part of the job for everyone is to keep each other hopeful. Part of the problem is that we don't really know how to tell good stories about the positive stuff and we do know how to tell stories about the really bad stuff. The more we pay attention to telling optimistic stories of our successes, the better chance we have of maintaining hope.

We often talk to groups who spend the whole day sharing really positive and hopeful insights, but who in the end need to be encouraged to see those successes for what they are. And they need to be reminded to celebrate all of their successes, too.

Free 4

Questions to discuss:

Do you ever find yourself losing hope? Are the stories that go around about the most recent disasters, or are they about the great things that happen?

Things to practice:

Practice telling upbeat and encouraging stories about the positive stuff. Let go of the negative stories. Give the people in your network permission to remind each other to stay positive and hopeful.

Things to try:

Focus on the positive, and don't forget to include the small things. For every negative or hopeless comment that escapes your mouth, make three hopeful comments.

Rather than dwelling on problems, focus on solutions!

Also remember, the more you are a part of your community, the more happy and hopeful you will become, so (have we said this before?) keep putting yourself out there.

Pay attention to non-verbal cues (85)

Think about the messages we're sending through our facial expressions and body posture.

How might you look more friendly and open?

Things to talk about:

We have talked already about using body language and facial expressions as a way to clarify what you are saying, and as a way to make your conversation partners feel relaxed. Re-member, most of communication is non-verbal. Your eyes, your smile, and your posture say more than words ever could.

But most non-verbal communication is subconscious. We all need to work at being more conscious of our non-verbal cues.

Questions to discuss:

What message do you think people are sending if they look down or look away while speaking to someone? Or if they stand with their arms crossed and a frown on their face?

If you look annoyed while telling a joke or making a comical remark, how do you think the person you're joking with might take it?

What kinds of non-verbal communication make us appear friendlier and more interested?

Things to practice:

In our workshops, we get folks to role play different types of non-verbal communication – closed off and unfriendly and open and inviting. Feel free to exaggerate a little to make things more concrete.

At home, ask the people in your network to let you know when your body language is making you seem closed off and unfriendly.

Smile, make eye contact and use body language in a way that puts your conversation partners at ease. Practice this with people you trust, and also in front of a mirror.

Things to try:

Whenever you are interacting with others, be aware of what you are saying with your non-verbal cues. Try to ensure that your verbal and non-verbal communication compliment one another.

Notice people with great social skills (86)

Who do you know who has lots of friends and seems comfortable in any situation?

If you can identify someone within your group with excellent social skills, try breaking down what it is that makes them so good at it. Ask yourself, what is it you see when you watch them interact with others?

Then ask that person, how would you help someone to improve their social skills?   You'll hear some interesting advice.

Learn from them.

Things to talk about:

Again, people with disabilities often have the best social skills.

Quite often, we have found that people with great social skills come from families with great social skills.

By noticing the folks you know with excellent social skills, you can

175

learn to improve your own.

Questions to discuss:

Why are good social skills important?

If fear of rejection is a part of the problem for you, how can you begin to get over that? Try writing down all the wonderful things you will gain in your life by overcoming this fear. This can be a powerful way to overcome these worries. Keep this list somewhere where you will see it regularly.

> **We need to move from the leader as hero, to the leader as host.**
>
> **Margaret Wheatley**

Things to practice:

Make a list of positive social skills. Some ideas are: inclusion; compassion; forgiveness; sense of humour; sharing; and cooperation. What else can you come up with?

Get into small groups and have each person say something nice about the others.

Things to try:

When you are out in the world, take note of those people who have great social skills. Some things you might notice about them are that they use friendly facial expressions and body language, they know how to give and receive compliments, they have good manners, they are nicely groomed, and they don't get upset easily.

Invite people over for a holiday meal (87)

Host Christmas dinner at your place this year – or find a

176

community meal for Thanksgiving and start a new tradition

"Invite a Neighbour for Dinner" day is the second Saturday in January

Things to talk about:

Inviting people over for holiday meals is a great way of deepening relationships. Eating together is a very intimate act, and often mealtime is the only time we slow down in our busy lives, and we only do that if we have an intention to slow down.

Let's face it; food tastes better when it is shared with good company. Organize that for your new and old friends during the holidays and they will be grateful to you.

Some of the benefits of shared meals are improved communication and social skills, improved table manners, and stronger networks.

Questions to discuss:

Which are your favourite holidays?

What do you like to cook?

How many people would you be comfortable having over for a holiday meal? Would you do all the cooking, or would you prefer a pot-luck style meal? Brunch, lunch or dinner?

Things to practice:

Look through some cookbooks, or go through your recipe files. Decide what you might make for your next holiday meal.

Think about how you might decorate your place and how you might arrange your table. Think about who you will invite.

177

Things to try:

Now you're ready to invite your friends and family. Give folks plenty of notice and let them know if you want them to bring anything. Get as much prepared ahead of time as you can, so that you can enjoy the company of your loved ones when they arrive.

Rake a neighbour's lawn, or shovel their snow (88)

Be the kind of person who does helpful things for your neighbours out of the kindness of your heart.

We often hear folks talking about how there is less feeling of community these days, especially in the big urban centres. But through one act of kindness at a time, we can change this. Sometimes, even in the most isolating of situations, you will see someone who is connected to everyone they pass. That's just a person like you or me who made a choice to do one thing at a time to connect with others.

Things to talk about:

The world needs more people who will do nice things for their neighbours without having to be asked, and without necessarily having to be thanked.

A healthy community needs

people whose custom it is to help each other and watch out for each other.

9 Cats and Virginia Woolf

Neighbours notice the community member who by their nature helps out their fellow man. In other words, neighbours notice their good neigh-bours.

Does it feel like community where you live?

Questions to discuss:

What could you do for your neighbours?

Are there seniors or a young family living near you who could use a little help?

Things to practice:

Make a list of things you could do in your neighbourhood. For example, take in the newspapers for a vacationing neighbour, or mow the boulevard for the family next door. What else can you think of?

Things to try:

Every time you get the chance; do something nice for a neighbour. In other words, do the neighbourly thing.

Afterwards, pause to think about how it felt to do something nice for your neighbours. How does being a good neighbour make you feel about yourself?

TIP: Add this to your list of affirmations – "I am a good neighbour!"

Recognize other people's accomplishments (89)

By recognising other people's accomplishments, we are telling them that we appreciate them. Don't just recognize major accomplishments, notice small things too.

Also, recognise accomplishments as they come – don't wait for a

179

birthday or other special event to pay someone a compliment on their achievements. Just notice what they are wearing, or what they did that was thoughtful. It's a way of being welcoming . . . one of the most welcoming people we know is Lorie, the President of B.C. People First – when Lorie welcomes you, you feel welcomed!

Things to talk about:

We tend to think more about recognizing accomplishments in the workplace, but people achieve goals, big and small, in all kinds of situations. What are some of the achieved goals that the group has seen that are examples of things they might talk about?

By taking note of the achievements of others, we make them feel good about themselves and increase our chances of friendship with them.

Questions to discuss:

What are the people around you accomplishing?

Why is it important to let people know we notice their successes?

Things to practice:

Try going around in a circle and taking turns complimenting people in the group by "tagging" them (and then they pick the next person). Shelley Nessman does a great variation of this by putting up cards (you could use sticky-notes) with people's "gifts" on them and having them claim their gifts. Once people have claimed something they feel good about, others could think of some way to recognise their gift.

Things to try:

Any time we notice someone's achievements, take time to recognize them. It will make them feel good, and it will make us feel good too,

180

and isn't this the foundation of friendship? Try going for a day (or a week) and not letting any opportunity to notice and talk about something we see people doing well pass us by.

Join a committee (90)

A Place at the Table

Organizations are always looking for people to sit on committees.

Things to talk about:

What is a committee? A committee is simply a group of people who get together to perform tasks on behalf of a larger organization. How many people in the group have been part of committees?

If folks have services through an agency, one way to start is to ask around at their agency about whether there are any committees they might join. Also they could ask the people in their networks.

Questions to discuss:

Does anyone in your group know of committees looking for members?

Things to practice:

Brainstorm a list of possible committees and decision-making

181

groups that folks could become a part of.

Here are some committee ideas to get you started: transit; gay pride; aboriginal; bicycle advisory; school board; community centre; library; community living.

Things to try:

Join a committee. Think about volunteering for the social arm of the committee you have chosen. Go to meetings – meet new friends while doing something good for your community!

Organize a fundraiser for the charity of your choice (91)

Often people think a fundraiser needs to be something big and complicated. Intead, they might pick something fun like a bake sale, and invite others to help – maybe Mrs. Smith from next door will donate some of her delicious double chocolate cookies...

Here is Susan's famous recipe for banana bread to get you started!

Ingredients
1 cup sugar
1/3 cup butter, soft
3 bananas (ripe)
2 eggs
1 tsp soda, dissolved in 1 Tbsp cold water
2 cups flour
1 tsp baking powder
1/2 tsp vanilla
1/4 tsp cinnamon
1/4 tsp nutmeg

Instructions
1. Heat oven to 350F
2. Combine and mix all ingredients together in a large mixing bowl.
3. Place batter in a greased bread pan (bottom only) or in muffin tins.
4. Bake 40 to 50 minutes or until wooden pick inserted in center comes out clean.
5. Cool for 10 minutes then remove from pan. Complete cooling on a wire rack

Makes one good sized loaf

Things to talk about:

Even if the person at the centre of the network can only run a spoon through the batter or pour the mix into the pan, they are still participating. This is a great time to discuss the idea of partial participation. Almost no one does anything completely alone . . . we all need a little help sometimes.

Questions to discuss:

Besides a bake sale, what are some other fundraising activities the group can think of?

Which charities would people choose to become involved with?

Things to practice:

Once they have decided on a charity, they might call the folks in their network to ask for help. They could get everyone together to discuss the details and plan the event. Make a list of the jobs that need to be done and ask for volunteers. Give plenty of time, so no one gets overwhelmed.

Be the person who remembers birthdays (92)

We have never met anyone as good at remember birthdays and other special events as self advocate leader Barb Goode. She sends cards and makes a point to contact people on their birthdays, which of course makes her friends and family feel loved and special.

She has friends all over the world who appreciate her thoughtfulness and whenever they meet her, they say "Thanks for that birthday card!"

Things to talk about:

The first thing to do is to collect the birthdays of all the folks in your network. Put the dates beside their name in your address book. Mark the dates on your calendar. If you have a computer or a smart phone, input the information into the calendar function and set it to remind you in advance. As you meet new people, ask them when their birthday is and add it to your collection. Ask: how will people do this?

Questions to discuss:

How does it make you feel when someone remembers your birthday or other special personal events like anniversaries?

How does it make you feel to be a person who makes a point of remembering birthdays?

Things to practice:

> "There is no higher purpose than service to others"
>
> **Dan Millman**

Have everyone in your group exchange birthday information.

184

In smaller groups, rehearse what you might say to friends when you make your birthday calls.

Buy or make cards for them. Think about making or buying your cards in advance so that you always have them ready.

If you are into crafts or baking, you could make something nice for your friends for their birthdays without having to spend a fortune. Do people have good stories about things they did for friends that were appreciated?

Join in the fun (93)

So, hopefully, people are getting out there into the world and going places where they have opportunities to meet new people. Fo some of us, the next step is to actually join in the fun! To not hang back and be a wallflower.

Things to talk about:

What's it like to be a wallflower?

There's no better way to connect with other people than to do something fun together. Whether we are looking to make one friend, or a hundred, we can assume that everyone wants to meet someone that they can have fun with.

Questions to discuss:

What do you enjoy doing? Where could you go where folks would be having your kind of fun?

185

Where you'd have a chance to show what you were comfortable with and good at?

What would be some of the benefits of open-ing yourself up to joining in on new activities?

Things to practice:

Get into groups of three or more and role play joining in on the fun. Pretend you're playing cards or a board game, and have each person from the group take a turn to be the one to be to join in. As the join-ee, walk up to the group, introduce yourself, and ask if you can play.

This can be hard for shy folks, so give them plenty of encouragement.

Things to try:

Decide that the next time you have the chance to join in on something fun, do it!   Don't wait for an invitation, just assume you're welcome and wanted (probably you are).   You will find that it gets easier every time you try.

Once you become a person who joins in on the fun, the next step is to become the type of person who invites others to join in.

TIP: If shyness is a problem for some of your group, Google 'overcoming shyness' for some great articles on the subject and maybe show some videos of people who are also working on this. Often people feel they are alone in this feeling. And they are NOT!

Host a potluck picnic (94)

Summer is a great time to host outdoor social events and a great season for picnics. Why not combine the two things into one. Host a potluck picnic! Of all hosted events this may be the simplest and the one people enjoy most.

Things to talk about:

Potluck meals are low-stress events where everyone pitches in. Picnics are a casual way to get some friends together. What park, beach or place might they gather some friends?

Questions to discuss:

Do they want to ask folks to bring specific food items or do you want to wing it? (The smaller the group the more you might want to know what people are bringing.) An easy way to deal with this is to take on making the main course (burgers or hot dogs perhaps) and ask people to bring salads and desserts.

Things to practice:

Make a list of people to invite. Decide whether you want to mail out invitations or call people on the phone. Choose an excellent picnic spot. If it seems like the weather might not cooperate, it might be wise to choose a place with an available covered area.

Things to try:

Invite the people on your list to your potluck picnic. If you mail out invitations, ask folks to RSVP. Give them a good two weeks notice. Make sure you tell them if you want them to bring a specific food item, or a generic item like dessert, main course, or salad. Also, tell them if they need to bring anything else, like drinks, lawn chairs, plates, cutlery, a barbecue, or a fun outdoor game.

Learn the art of small talk (95)

"How are you?"

"What do you think of this weather?"

Have the group think of a few phrases to get past the initial "hello"

Things to talk about:

Small talk really is an art in the sense that it takes some creativity to become an expert.

Questions to discuss:

Some people are excellent at starting conversations. Think about people you know who are good at the art of small talk. What makes them so good at it? Are there any folks in your group who are good at small talk? Have them share some pointers. If they're comfortable have them role-play meeting someone new and then discuss what people saw. David Pitonyak does a thing where he says "freeze" as people role-play and then the group discusses what they saw.

Things to practice:

Brainstorm a list of possible topics for small talk. Break up into pairs and practice your small talk.

At home, make a point of rehearsing light conversation starters with the people in your networks.

Things to try:

Whenever you run into someone, whether it's someone new or someone you already know, practice your small talk. Try to keep the conversation going, but don't worry if it doesn't. Sometimes, a little small talk is all the situation calls for. Very few people seem to feel they're good at this, even if we think they are!

TIPS: The 'art' in the art of small talk is being able to branch out from your original topic. If you are talking about the weather, for instance, you could branch out into a conversation about the worst weather you have ever experienced, which could turn into a chat about vacations. You get the picture.

So... You want to get romantic? (96)

Having a boyfriend or girlfriend involves a whole other set of skills that no-one is born knowing . . . but it might be the most important thing to the folks in your group, or to some of them. It might be the reason they wanted to talk about this.

One good way to begin is to talk to people they know and trust and find out how other singles in the area meet people. It can really change from place to place.

Things to talk about:

As supporters of folks with disabilities, we need to remind ourselves often that we are all human and for the most part we all have the same basic wants and needs. Most humans pair-bond – that is, we tend to form long lasting monogamous relationships. We fall in love, get married and have kids.

Everyone who has come to us over the years and said that they want a boyfriend or girlfriend, husband or wife, has gotten those things, or gotten close to getting those things, by expanding their social networks. Most of us meet our potential partners through our work-mates and our friends.

This can be one of the hardest things to facilitate, but it can also be a lot of fun.

This is a great time to discuss sexual orientation and to teach safe sex practices. Give this lots of time. Find a local authority if you feel uncomfortable.

Questions to discuss:

Ask the folks in your group how many of them would like to meet someone and fall in love. How many in your group are in relationships? Ask them for their advice. Do they know of anyone who met someone and got romantic before they knew how to make friends?

Things to practice:

Have a discussion about where to meet potential boyfriends/girlfriends and come up with a list.

This is a great time to practice the art of small talk, and to practice introducing yourself. Work at getting over any nervousness and fear of rejection.

Many of us already know someone that we would like to get to know better, we may just need to overcome our anxiety.

Things to try:

Go to the next dance or party and introduce yourself to other singles. If it feels right, ask someone you're interested in whether they would like to meet you for a coffee or a movie. Take things slowly and see where they go!

Set goals (97)

Facilitate a realistic hopefulness. Remember Norman Kunc's essay, "Being realistic isn't realistic!" Write down goals for people in some way that they can take with them (the chance of success greatly increases) – sticky notes are great.

If all you want is a quiet companion to take long hikes with, and you find one, your goal is accomplished . . . no-one else can say how many friends you need, or what your relationships *should* look like

Things to talk about:

Often people talk about SMART goals - specific, measurable, realistic, attainable and time-targeted. This can be a lot to explain and expect the first time round, so gauge the capacity of your group. Goals can generally be about anything we want, but for the purposes of this book we are talking about friendship goals and, already, one of the things that we'll be dealing with is the assumption that "friends just happen." Or, for many people, "friends just happen – to good people – so there must be something wrong with me."

An idea can be to talk about not beating oneself up if a goal is not achieved. Instead, take it as an opportunity to sit down with the people in their network and discuss what went wrong. Most often people don't give themselves enough time. Or we set goals that are too hard – these are the goals that should be broken down into more 'doable' portions.

Remember too, that sometimes our goals change as we're going along, and that's perfectly okay.

Questions to discuss:

What are some common friendship goals? What do we assume

191

everyone wants in friends?

What are some different ways that goals can be written down? Or drawn?

What it the best way to write goals so that the person at the centre of the network can easily understand and keep track of them?

Things to practice:

Have each person in your group come up with one goal. Then talk about what it's like to have a goal, what different ways could you use to remind yourself of your goal, and who you could enlist to help you to succeed.

Later, get your support network together and come up with some more goals around friendship. Write them down.

Things to try:

As people work towards their goals, they might want to figure out a way to track their progress. Some people use a calendar, while others use a journal or a day planner – the key is to find a system that works for each of us.

Imagine a future with friends (98)

Where will you be in 5 years? 10 years? Who will be your friends then?

Things to talk about:

This is an exercise in hope and positive thinking. In imagining a future with friends, we allow ourselves to dream of a perfect life. In PATHs Jack Pierpoint and Marsha Forest used to "plan backwards" by having people close their eyes and imagine "well, the date is (a year from now) and the last year went really, really well... let's remember everything we did in the last year! What did you do right after we met and did that PATH last year?"

Questions to discuss:

When imagining their futures with friends, what does it look like? How many friends would they like to have? What might change to make that happen (or, what might have changed?)? Do they imagine one really close friend, or many? What kinds of things would they do together?

Things to practice:

What we often do here with our groups is a simple guided meditation. Get folks to relax their feet and then slowly relax the muscles all the way up their bodies to the tops of their heads. Name each part. "Let your toes relax, let the stress go, and now your feet, let your feet relax... and now your calves – imagine the stress rising up and leaving your calves..." Go to the top of the head and then suggest they let the stress just rise up out of their skulls and into the sky, not to return. Very often people with disabilities haven't had a lot of experience with relaxation! Go slow, take your time. Now that everyone is relaxed, get them to imagine 5 years into the future. Get them to imagine that they are surrounded by friends. It could be a birthday party and all their friends are there. Ask them to think about who would be there and what they are like. For example, what will your friends be doing for fun and for work?

Bring them slowly out out of the meditation ("When you are ready, open your eyes, look around, and come back to the group.") and talk about what they could do now to get ready for their imagined future with friends.

The more we consciously think about a future with friends, the deeper it seeps into our subconscious mind. And the more these

193

thoughts enter our subconscious, the greater the chance of our dreams coming true. Over time, you will find that you become increasingly aware of friendship opportunities, and that you are better prepared to take full advantage of the opportunities when they arise. This is akin to the power of positive thinking!

Things to try:

Allow yourself to imagine a future with friends and be prepared to have your dreams come true.

See yourself as a community builder (90)

All over the world people are trying to create community. YOU are part of this, a leader, and people with disabilities know more about leading the world in regaining quality of life than almost any other group, because they've been thinking about it more consciously, for longer.

Things to talk about:

By making the decision to increase your personal support network, you have in fact made a decision to strengthen your community. You are already a community builder!

It's true that many of today's strongest community builders are folks with disabilities.

Questions to discuss:

How do people build community?

On a personal level, how do we keep ourselves hopeful and happy as we work towards strengthening our communities?

Things to practice:

Brainstorm a list of ways that the people in your group are already

194

community builders. Think in terms of the gifts folks have for improving the quality of life of those around them.

Expand your list with new ideas for strengthening your community.

Things to try:

We build community by being a part of community. Go out and meet your neighbours, use your library, welcome newcomers, be helpful, share what you can, sing together, shop in your neighbourhood, respect senior citizens and different cultures, believe in equality for all – in short, be a good neighbour, a good person, and a good friend.

Make the most of each new day (100)

> Yesterday is history
> tomorrow is a mystery
> today is a gift –
> that's why it's called "the present"

Things to talk about:

The above poem may be a little cheesy, but it is true. Yesterday is gone and tomorrow never comes. Today is all we really have, so to be happy in our lives we need to make the most of it. John McGee, who we have worked with in the past, used to say "In our field we do a great job of planning the future, a not bad job of documenting the past, but a really bad job of

> "Sometimes you wake up. Sometimes the fall kills you. And sometimes, when you fall, you fly."
>
> **Neil Gaiman**

this moment!"

The folks we support have often been victimised by focusing on the mistakes they may have made in the past, and promised that their dreams would be taken seriously... but instead they get turned into goal statements. Don't let any of us get to the end of our lives wishing we had fulfilled our dreams.

Again, this is about the power of positive thinking, but it is also about the power of positive doing. Another common saying is, 'The way you spend your day is the way you spend your life.'

Questions to discuss:

What would help you to make the most of each new day?

Children are excellent at making the most of each day. How do they do it?

Things to practice:

Make a list of ideas for making the most of this day, today. What happened since people woke up that was good?

Have folks think about when they were children. Kids let themselves dream big. Discuss childhood passions. Often, thinking about our childhood passions helps us to get in touch with what currently makes us happy. Be childlike in your imaginings.

Things to try:

All day long, remind yourself to live each moment as if it were your last. Turn it into an affirmation: 'I will live each day to the fullest!'

Be honest with yourself about what truly makes you happy, and ensure that you live your life according to your own values – not values that other people think you should live by.

One last anonymous quote: 'Dream as if you'll live forever, live as if you'll die tomorrow.'

_____ **(101)**

Well, you now have 100 concrete ideas for ways to make new friends!

This is your chance to add to the list. In our workshops we have gotten as high as 132 before we ran out of time. Speaking of time, you might have to put a time limit on this exercise, because the folks in your group have been waiting so patiently to share their ideas and they most likely have plenty of them.   Pay attention. Listen.   Write down everyone's ideas.   Perhaps even draw them!

A Short List of Selected Resources

101 Friends Project and Spectrum Press @ www.101friends.ca

Peter Block, *Community: Structures for Belonging.*

C.L.B.C. Resources www.communitylivingbc.ca and search for publications – some great things to download

John T. Cacioppo and William Patrick *Loneliness: Human Nature and the Need for Social Connection* http://scienceofloneliness.com/

Jack Canfield. The author and editor of the Chicken Soup for the Soul books, Canfield is also the writer of *The Success Principles* – a great resource for thinking about planning and aspiration.

Peggy Hutchinson and John Lord, with Karen Lord. *Friends and Inclusion: Five Approaches to Building Relationships.* This is one of the several books by John Lord and Peggy Hutchinson.

Inclusion Press www.inclusion.com

Norman Kunc & Emma Van der Klift www.normemma.com - like John Lord, Norm and Emma are under-recognised national treasures

David Pitonyak can be found at www.dimagine.com

Rock Paper Scissors http://blog.rpsinc.ca

The companion volume on which this facilitators' manual is based, *101 Ways To Make Friends: Ideas and Conversation Starters for People with Disabilities and Their Supporters*, is published by Spectrum Press, a division of Spectrum Society

www.spectrumsociety.org

Subscribe to our blog / newsletter
Or check out new publications here:
www.101friends.ca
To find us on facebook, search on "Spectrum"
Tweet us @101FriendsBC or @SSCLSpectrum
Or, for Aaron, @imagineacircle

The ideas in this book are based on many conversations with folks with disabilities, individually and as part of groups like People First, their friends, families and teams that have all shared with us their expertise, dreams and goals and in the process have made us part of their networks, for which we are grateful.

Our e-newsletter and blog are an attempt to keep these conversations going and connect those who think this is vitally important work: check out www.101friends.ca   Everyone has great stories about how they made friends. Maybe you've done something that others could learn from – we'd love to hear from you!

Email us at psn@spectrumsociety.org

About the authors

Susan Stanfield
Director, Communications and Quality Assurance
Spectrum Society for Community Living

Susan has worked in community living for nearly 30 years. She coordinated recreation programs and volunteer services for the Autism Society of B.C. while attending university, and worked for a number of local community agencies prior to co-founding Spectrum Society in 1987. As a co-director of Spectrum, Susan oversees the information management and infrastructure that supports Spectrum's services to individuals and families in the greater Vancouver area. She lives in Burnaby with her two sons.

Aaron Johannes
Director of Research, Training and Development
Spectrum Society for Community Living

Aaron is a Co-Director of Spectrum and a proud family member to people with disabilities. He and his partner have been foster-parents for more than a dozen years to teens with significant challenges and also have a young son; among various other roles he has been gratified to learn from he has been a facilitator with the Vela Microboard Association and a writer. He is a provincial advisor for People First, which he considers his avocation, and his passions are art, literature, alternative health, business philosophy and gardening. He has exhibited his work in juried exhibitions as well as publications. He is currently working on a Masters degree in Equity Studies with a focus on the support of people with intellectual disabilities in participatory community leadership.

Jim Reynolds
Manager, Social Enterprises
Spectrum Society for Community Living

Jim has worked in social services for more than 25 years. He started out working in an outreach service for seniors living in Vancouver's downtown eastside, and has been a manager for Spectrum Society since 1990. Jim lives in Vancouver with his partner and their two cats. His passions are writing, reading and jazz music. He hosts a book collecting website at www.jamespreynolds.com and has written three novels. He is also proud to have assisted disability rights activist Barb Goode to write her autobiography *The Goode Life*.

Spectrum Press

A DIVISION OF SPECTRUM SOCIETY
FOR COMMUNITY LIVING

Spectrum Press publishes approximately
five books and/or DVDs each year
by, with or about self-advocates, self-determination,
support networks and best-practices

The 101 Friends Project
conducts community based research projects
facilitates and hosts workshops
and encourages person-centred best practices
and partnership

To learn more about our work
visit www.101friends.ca
or www.spectrumsociety.org

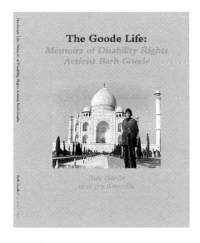

Publication Date May 2011
The long awaited *The Goode Life:*
Memoirs of Disability Rights Activist
Barb Goode, **by Barb Goode with Jim**
Reynolds

Order it through your local bookshop,
lulu.com, amazon (internationally), or
www.101friends.ca

Susan, Aaron and Jim have facilitated workshops and taught classes over much of the continent on support networks, instructional strategies, the changing role of community supports and other topics. They have also worked with groups of self-advocates to translate government documents into graphics and plain language.

Feedback from participants:

"Thank you for an excellent workshop. It will help us on our uncharted journey to support my son."

"Presented in an easy to understand format (with simple language)."

"Great day, thank you!" "Best workshop ever!" "I had fun, I learned how to make friends." "Please come back." (Self-advocate feedback.)

"You spread hopefulness in the universe; the question isn't whether the glass is half empty or half full, it is how 'how do we fill up the glass?'"

The overwhelmingly positive evaluations are a testament to your hard work. Thank you so much!"

For more information about workshops, publications, events or other speakers we host please contact psn@spectrumsociety.org or visit us at www.101friends.ca